Praise for Stucki's Books: "Concise reads.  Extreme value!"

# Stand Out!

## 15 No-Hype Strategies

## Get Noticed and Get Ahead

A Keys of Knowledge Book

By H. Bradley Stucki

# Who Should Read This Book

Are you ready to take your career to the next level? Do you want to stand out from the crowd and get noticed for all the right reasons? If you're nodding your head (or even if you're just mildly curious), then congratulations! You've picked up the right book.

"Stand Out! 15 No-Hype Strategies; Get Noticed and Get Ahead" is for anyone who wants to shine in their professional life, regardless of where they are on their career journey. But let's get a bit more specific, shall we?

**This book is perfect for:**

1. **The Ambitious Newcomer**: Just starting your career and want to make a splash? These strategies will help you build a strong foundation and get noticed right from the get-go.

2. **The Mid-Career Professional**: Feeling stuck in your current role? These pages hold the keys to reigniting your career and standing out in a sea of competent colleagues.

3. **The Seasoned Expert**: Even if you're at the top of your game, there's always room for growth. Discover new ways to leverage your experience and continue to stand out in your field.

4. **The Career Changer**: Switching gears to a new industry or role? These strategies will help you transfer your skills and make a strong impression in your new field.

5. **The Entrepreneur**: Whether you're a solopreneur or leading a startup, standing out is crucial for your business success. These strategies apply just as much to building your business as they do to building your career.

6. **The Freelancer**: In the gig economy, standing out is everything. Learn how to differentiate yourself and become the go-to professional in your niche.

7. **The Remote Worker**: In a virtual work environment, it can be challenging to get noticed. These strategies will help you shine, even through a screen.

8. **The Leader**: If you're managing a team or aspiring to do so, these strategies will not only help you stand out but also inspire and elevate those around you.

9. **The Lifelong Learner**: If you're always on the lookout for new ways to grow and improve, you'll find plenty of food for thought and action in these pages.

But here's the thing: this book isn't just for people with specific job titles or years of experience. It's for anyone who believes that they have more to offer, anyone who wants to make a bigger impact in their professional life, anyone who's ever thought, "I know I can do more, be more, achieve more."

It's for the quiet genius who wants to finally be heard, the hard worker who wants their efforts to be recognized, the creative thinker who wants to see their ideas implemented.

It's for you if you've ever felt overlooked, undervalued, or stuck in a rut.

It's for you if you're doing well but know you could be doing even better.

It's for you if you want to not just succeed, but truly excel in your career.

In short, if you picked up this book, it's for you.

So, whether you're reading this in a corner office with a view, a bustling coffee shop as you build your side hustle, or curled up on your couch dreaming of your next career move, know that you're in the right place.

The strategies in this book are designed to be practical, actionable, and adaptable to wherever you are in your professional journey. They're not about flashy gimmicks or overnight success. They're about building a solid foundation for long-term career success and fulfillment.

Ready to stand out and get ahead? Let's dive in!

# My Promise to You - the Reader

Welcome, ambitious professional! You've taken the first step towards transforming your career by picking up this book. Now, before we dive into the strategies that will help you stand out and get ahead, I want to make a few promises to you. Consider this our professional pact, if you will.

**Here's what I promise this book will deliver:**

1. **No Fluff, Just Substance**: I promise to respect your time and intelligence. Each chapter is packed with actionable insights and practical strategies. No filler, no unnecessary jargon, just solid, usable content.

2. **Real-World Applicability**: These aren't just theories that sound good on paper. Every strategy in this book has been battle-tested in the real world. I promise you'll find ideas you can start implementing immediately, regardless of your industry or career stage.

3. **Honesty and Transparency**: I won't sugarcoat things or promise overnight success. Standing out takes effort and time. But I promise to be upfront about what it takes and to provide you with a clear roadmap for getting there.

4. **Inclusivity**: Whether you're an introvert or extrovert, entry-level or executive, working in tech or teaching, there's something here for you. I promise strategies that can be adapted to various personalities, work styles, and career paths.

5. **Empowerment, Not Dependency**: My goal isn't to make you reliant on this book, but to empower you with tools and mindsets that you can use independently. I promise to teach you how to fish, not just hand you a fish.

6. **Ethical Strategies**: In a world where it can sometimes seem like the loudest or most aggressive get ahead, I promise to focus on ethical, sustainable strategies that allow you to succeed while maintaining your integrity.

7. **Continual Growth**: These strategies aren't a one-and-done deal. I promise to show you how to use these tools for ongoing professional development, helping you adapt and thrive in an ever-changing work landscape.

8. **Balance of Inspiration and Practicality**: While I'll provide plenty of motivational fuel, I promise not to rely on hype or empty cheerleading. You'll find a healthy balance of inspiration and concrete, actionable steps.

9. **Acknowledgment of Challenges**: I promise not to gloss over the difficulties you might face. We'll address common obstacles head-on and provide strategies for overcoming them.

10. **Respect for Your Unique Journey**: Your career path is yours alone. I promise to provide strategies flexible enough to be tailored to your unique goals, values, and circumstances.

11. **A Touch of Humor**: While we're dealing with serious career strategies, I promise to keep things light where appropriate. After all, if we can't enjoy the journey, what's the point?

12. **An Open Dialogue**: Though a book is inherently one-sided, I promise to write in a way that feels like a conversation. I'll anticipate your questions and address them as we go along.

13. **Value Beyond the Last Page**: The strategies in this book aren't meant to be read and forgotten. I promise to provide tools and insights that you'll find yourself returning to throughout your career.

14. **No-Hype Zone**: As the title suggests, I promise to steer clear of over-hyped, get-successful-quick schemes. We're here for sustainable, long-term success.

15. **A Call to Action**: Lastly, I promise to challenge you. Reading this book is just the start. I'll encourage you to reflect, to plan, and most importantly, to act.

Remember, this book is a tool, and like any tool, its true value lies in how you use it. I've done my part by distilling years of experience and research into these pages. Now, it's over to you.

Are you ready to stand out and get ahead? Let's get started on this exciting journey together!

# Introduction: Your Path to Standing Out and Getting Ahead

In today's hyper-competitive professional landscape, simply being good at your job is no longer enough. To truly thrive and advance in your career, you need to stand out from the crowd. But how exactly do you do that without resorting to shameless self-promotion or gimmicks? That's precisely what this book is all about.

Welcome to "Stand Out! 15 No-Hype Strategies; Get Noticed and Get Ahead." If you're holding this book, chances are you're ready to take your career to the next level. Maybe you're feeling stuck in your current role, or perhaps you're doing well but know you have the potential to achieve even more. Whatever your situation, you've come to the right place.

In the pages that follow, we'll explore 15 proven strategies that will help you differentiate yourself, showcase your unique value, and advance your career. These aren't quick fixes or flashy tricks. They're substantive, ethical approaches that will not only help you stand out but will also make you a better professional in the process.

Each chapter focuses on a specific strategy, providing you with:

1. A clear explanation of the strategy and why it's important
2. Practical tips for implementing the strategy in your daily work life
3. Real-world examples of how others have successfully used this approach
4. Potential challenges you might face and how to overcome them
5. Actionable steps you can take to start applying the strategy right away

We'll cover a wide range of topics, from developing unique skills and delivering consistently high-quality work, to mastering the art of strategic networking and personal branding. We'll delve into the importance of continuous learning, the power of mentoring others, and the crucial role of adaptability in today's ever-changing work environment.

But this book is more than just a collection of strategies. It's a roadmap for professional growth and success. As you progress through the chapters, you'll notice how these strategies interconnect and reinforce each other, creating a comprehensive approach to career advancement.

One of the beauties of these strategies is their flexibility. Whether you're a fresh graduate just starting your career, a mid-level manager looking to climb the corporate ladder, or an entrepreneur building your own business, you'll find valuable insights that you can adapt to your unique situation.

Remember, standing out isn't about being the loudest or the most aggressive. It's about consistently demonstrating your value, building meaningful relationships, and continually growing and adapting. It's about being authentically you, but the best professional version of you possible.

As we embark on this journey together, I encourage you to approach each chapter with an open mind and a willingness to step out of your comfort zone. Some strategies might come naturally to you, while others might challenge you. Embrace both. Growth often happens when we push ourselves beyond what's comfortable.

Also, keep in mind that change doesn't happen overnight. Implementing these strategies is a process, not an event. Be patient with yourself, celebrate small wins along the way, and remember that every step forward, no matter how small, is progress.

Are you ready to stand out and get ahead? Are you ready to unlock your full professional potential? Then let's dive in. Your journey to becoming a standout professional starts now. Turn the page, and let's begin with Strategy #1: Develop a Unique Skill or Expertise.

Welcome to your future success story. Let's make it remarkable!

# Chapter 1: Develop a Unique Skill or Expertise

In today's fast-paced and competitive world, being good at your job is no longer enough. To truly stand out and get ahead, you need to bring something special to the table. That's where developing a unique skill or expertise comes in. It's like having a secret weapon in your professional arsenal – one that sets you apart from the crowd and makes people sit up and take notice.

## The Power of Specialization

Think of your career as a vast ocean. In this metaphor, most professionals are generalists, swimming around in the shallows. They know a little bit about a lot of things, which is great for flexibility but not so great for standing out. Now, imagine diving deep into a specific area of your field. That's where the treasure lies!

By developing a unique skill or expertise, you become the go-to person for that particular niche. You're no longer just another fish in the sea; you're the expert on coral reefs or deep-sea creatures. People will seek you out for your knowledge and skills, giving you a significant edge in your career.

## Finding Your Niche

So, how do you find that special skill or area of expertise? Here are a few strategies to get you started:

1. **Follow Your Passion**: What aspects of your job or industry truly excite you? What could you talk about for hours without getting bored? Your passion is often a great indicator of where you should focus your efforts.

2. **Identify Gaps**: Look for areas in your field that are underserved or emerging. Is there a new technology that few people understand? A problem that needs solving? These gaps are opportunities for you to fill.

3. **Leverage Your Strengths**: What are you naturally good at? Your unique combination of skills and experiences might lead you to a specialization that others haven't considered.

4. **Stay Curious**: Keep an open mind and always be learning. Sometimes, your niche finds you when you least expect it.

## Cultivating Your Expertise

Once you've identified your area of focus, it's time to dive in and become the expert. Here's how:

### 1. Deep Learning

Immerse yourself in your chosen area. Read books, take courses, attend workshops, and seek out mentors. The goal is to know your niche inside and out.

For example, let's say you're in marketing and you've decided to specialize in neuromarketing – the application of neuroscience to marketing. You might start by reading foundational texts like "Neuromarketing" by Patrick Renvoisé and Christophe Morin [1], then move on to more specialized research papers and case studies.

### 2. Practice, Practice, Practice

Knowledge is great, but expertise comes from application. Look for opportunities to put your learning into practice, even if it means volunteering or doing side projects.

Continuing with our neuromarketing example, you might offer to help a local non-profit with their marketing efforts, applying your newfound knowledge to real-world situations.

3. Share Your Knowledge

Teaching others is one of the best ways to solidify your own understanding and establish yourself as an expert. Start a blog, create videos, or offer to speak at industry events.

4. Network with Fellow Experts

Connect with others who share your interests. Join professional associations, participate in online forums, and attend conferences in your niche. These connections can lead to collaborations, job opportunities, and further learning.

**The Compounding Effect of Expertise**

As you develop your unique skill or expertise, you'll likely notice a compounding effect. The more you learn and practice, the faster you'll acquire new related skills and knowledge. This is what author Scott H. Young calls "ultralearning" in his book of the same name [2].

Moreover, your growing expertise will open doors to new opportunities. You might be invited to contribute to industry publications, speak at conferences, or consult on high-profile projects. Each of these experiences further cements your status as an expert and helps you stand out even more.

## Balancing Depth and Breadth

While specialization is powerful, it's important to maintain a balance. You don't want to become so narrowly focused that you lose sight of the bigger picture or become obsolete if your niche disappears.

The key is to develop what author David Epstein calls "range" in his book "Range: Why Generalists Triumph in a Specialized World" [3]. While you have your area of deep expertise, continue to cultivate a broad base of knowledge and skills. This combination of depth and breadth will make you truly invaluable.

## Evolving Your Expertise

Remember, developing a unique skill or expertise isn't a one-time event – it's an ongoing process. As your field evolves, so should your knowledge. Stay curious, keep learning, and be ready to pivot or expand your expertise as needed.

## Conclusion

In a world where everyone is trying to stand out, developing a unique skill or expertise is your ticket to rising above the noise. It's not about becoming famous or being the loudest voice in the room. It's about bringing real value to your field and becoming the person people turn to when they need someone who really knows their stuff.

So, what's your niche going to be? What unique skill or expertise will you develop to stand out from the crowd? The journey starts now, and the only limit is your curiosity and determination. Dive deep, learn voraciously, and watch as doors of opportunity swing open for you.

Remember, in the words of author Robert Greene, "The future belongs to those who learn more skills and combine them in creative ways" [4]. So go forth, find your unique combination of skills, and make your mark on the world!

---

References:

[1] Renvoisé, P., & Morin, C. (2007). Neuromarketing: Understanding the Buy Buttons in Your Customer's Brain. Thomas Nelson.

[2] Young, S. H. (2019). Ultralearning: Master Hard Skills, Outsmart the Competition, and Accelerate Your Career. Harper Business.

[3] Epstein, D. (2019). Range: Why Generalists Triumph in a Specialized World. Riverhead Books.

[4] Greene, R. (2012). Mastery. Viking.

# Chapter 2: Consistently Deliver High-Quality Work

In a world where mediocrity often seems to be the norm, consistently delivering high-quality work is like having a superpower. It's the kind of thing that makes people sit up, take notice, and say, "Wow, who did this?" And before you know it, you're the person everyone wants on their team.

## The Power of Consistency

Let's face it: anyone can have a good day. You might hit a home run on a project once in a blue moon and bask in the glow of praise. But what really sets the superstars apart is their ability to knock it out of the park day after day, week after week.

Consistency in delivering high-quality work is like compound interest for your career. Each excellent piece of work builds on the last, creating a reputation that becomes increasingly valuable over time. As Warren Buffett once said, "It takes 20 years to build a reputation and five minutes to ruin it" [1]. So let's focus on building that reputation, shall we?

## Defining 'High-Quality'

Before we dive into the how-to, let's talk about what we mean by 'high-quality'. It's not about perfection – chasing that elusive goal is a surefire way to burn out faster than a candle in a windstorm. Instead, think of high-quality work as:

1. Meeting or exceeding expectations
2. Attention to detail
3. Thoughtfulness and creativity in approach
4. Timeliness
5. Usefulness or value to the end-user

## The High-Quality Mindset

Delivering consistently high-quality work starts with adopting the right mindset. Here are some key attitudes to cultivate:

1. Take Pride in Your Work

Approach each task, no matter how small, as a reflection of your personal brand. As Walt Disney said, "Whatever you do, do it well. Do it so well that when people see you do it, they will want to come back and see you do it again, and they will want to bring others and show them how well you do what you do" [2].

## 2. Embrace the Growth Mindset

View challenges as opportunities to learn and improve, not as obstacles. This concept, popularized by psychologist Carol Dweck in her book "Mindset: The New Psychology of Success," can transform how you approach your work [3].

## 3. Be Your Own Quality Control

Don't wait for others to catch your mistakes. Develop a keen eye for detail and a habit of self-review. As the old carpentry adage goes, "Measure twice, cut once."

**Strategies for Consistent Quality**

Now that we've got our mindset right, let's look at some practical strategies for consistently delivering high-quality work:

## 1. Develop a Personal Quality Checklist

Create a checklist of quality standards for your work. This could include things like:

- Is this my best effort?
- Have I double-checked for errors?
- Does this meet or exceed the requirements?
- Is there any way I could improve this?

Use this checklist before considering any piece of work complete. Over time, this process will become second nature.

## 2. Seek Feedback and Act on It

Don't wait for your annual review to find out how you're doing. Regularly ask for feedback from colleagues, supervisors, and even clients. And here's the kicker – actually use that feedback to improve. As Bill Gates said, "We all need people who will give us feedback. That's how we improve" [4].

## 3. Continuous Learning and Improvement

Stay up-to-date with the latest developments in your field. Attend workshops, read industry publications, or take online courses. The more you know, the better equipped you'll be to deliver top-notch work.

## 4. Time Management and Organization

High-quality work requires adequate time and mental space. Use productivity techniques like the Pomodoro Technique or time-blocking to ensure you're giving each task the attention it deserves [5].

## 5. Take Care of Yourself

You can't pour from an empty cup. Maintain a healthy work-life balance, get enough sleep, and take breaks. A refreshed mind is more likely to produce quality work.

## Case Study: The Pixar Approach

Let's look at a real-world example of consistently high-quality work: Pixar Animation Studios. Pixar has released 23 feature films as of 2021, and every single one has been a critical and commercial success. How do they do it?

According to Ed Catmull, co-founder of Pixar, in his book "Creativity, Inc.," their success comes down to a few key principles [6]:

1. Trust the process: Pixar has a well-defined process for creating films, which includes extensive storyboarding and numerous iterations.

2. Embrace failure: They view early failures as part of the process of achieving excellence.

3. Be candid: They have a "Braintrust" where team members give honest feedback on works in progress.

4. Constantly improve: They conduct postmortems after each film to learn and improve for the next one.

By adhering to these principles, Pixar has built a reputation for consistently delivering high-quality work that resonates with audiences worldwide.

## The Ripple Effect of Quality

When you consistently deliver high-quality work, you create a positive ripple effect:

1. **Trust**: People learn they can rely on you, which often leads to more autonomy and exciting opportunities.

2. **Inspiration**: Your high standards can inspire your colleagues to up their game, improving the overall quality of your team or organization.

3. **Personal Satisfaction**: There's an intrinsic reward in knowing you've done your best work.

4. **Career Advancement**: High-quality work often leads to recognition, which can translate into promotions or new career opportunities.

## Overcoming Obstacles

Of course, consistently delivering high-quality work isn't always easy. You might face tight deadlines, unclear expectations, or resource constraints. Here are a few strategies for overcoming these obstacles:

1. **Communicate**: If you're facing constraints that might impact quality, communicate early and often with stakeholders.

2. **Prioritize**: When time is tight, focus on the most critical aspects of the project.

3. **Seek Help**: Don't be afraid to ask for help or resources when you need them.

4. **Learn to Say No**: Sometimes, maintaining quality means turning down projects that you don't have the capacity to do well.

## Conclusion

Consistently delivering high-quality work isn't about being perfect. It's about committing to excellence in everything you do, learning from your mistakes, and constantly striving to improve. It's a marathon, not a sprint, but the rewards – both personal and professional – are well worth the effort.

Remember, in the words of Aristotle, "We are what we repeatedly do. Excellence, then, is not an act, but a habit" [7]. So go forth and make excellence your habit. Your future self (and your career) will thank you for it!

---

References:

[1] Buffett, W. (2006). Letter to Berkshire Hathaway Shareholders.

[2] Disney, W. (attributed). Various sources.

[3] Dweck, C. S. (2006). Mindset: The New Psychology of Success. Random House.

[4] Gates, B. (attributed). Various sources.

[5] Cirillo, F. (2006). The Pomodoro Technique. FC Garage.

[6] Catmull, E., & Wallace, A. (2014). Creativity, Inc.: Overcoming the Unseen Forces That Stand in the Way of True Inspiration. Random House.

[7] Durant, W. (1926). The Story of Philosophy. Simon & Schuster. (Note: This quote is often misattributed to Aristotle, but it's actually Will Durant's interpretation of Aristotle's philosophy)

# Chapter 3: Be Punctual and Reliable

In a world where time is money and trust is gold, being punctual and reliable is like having a secret key to success. It might not sound as flashy as being a creative genius or a visionary leader, but let me tell you, it's a superpower that can take you places you never imagined.

### The Power of Punctuality and Reliability

Think about it: When was the last time you were impressed by someone who was consistently late or always dropped the ball? Probably never. Now, think about the people you admire most in your professional life. Chances are, they're the ones you can set your watch by and trust with your most important tasks.

Being punctual and reliable is like wearing an invisible badge that says, "I've got this." It's a simple yet powerful way to stand out from the crowd and build a reputation that opens doors.

### The Cost of Being Late and Unreliable

Before we dive into how to be punctual and reliable, let's take a moment to consider the flip side. A study by salary.com found that tardiness costs U.S. companies more than $3 billion annually in lost productivity [1]. But the cost isn't just financial – it's personal too.

When you're consistently late or unreliable, you're sending a message (whether you intend to or not) that you don't value other people's time or trust. Over time, this can erode relationships, damage your reputation, and limit your opportunities.

## The Punctuality Mindset

Being punctual starts with adopting the right mindset. Here are some key attitudes to cultivate:

### 1. Respect for Time

View time as a precious, non-renewable resource – both yours and others'. As Benjamin Franklin famously said, "Lost time is never found again" [2].

### 2. Commitment to Promises

See every commitment, no matter how small, as a promise. And promises are meant to be kept.

## 3. Proactive Planning

Adopt a mindset of "If I'm not early, I'm late." This buffer can be a lifesaver when unexpected delays occur.

## Strategies for Punctuality

Now, let's look at some practical strategies to boost your punctuality game:

## 1. The 15-Minute Rule

Always aim to arrive 15 minutes early for appointments and deadlines. This buffer time can absorb unexpected delays and give you a chance to collect your thoughts.

## 2. Realistic Time Estimation

Most people underestimate how long tasks will take. This phenomenon, known as the "planning fallacy," was identified by psychologists Daniel Kahneman and Amos Tversky [3].

Combat this by tracking how long tasks actually take and using this data for future planning.

## 3. Prepare in Advance

Lay out your clothes, pack your bag, and gather necessary materials the night before. This reduces morning stress and helps you start the day on time.

## 4. Use Technology Wisely

Set multiple alarms, use calendar apps with reminders, and leverage GPS for accurate travel times. But remember, technology is a tool, not a crutch.

## 5. The Power of "No"

Learn to say no to commitments you can't realistically meet. It's better to decline upfront than to overcommit and underdeliver.

**The Reliability Factor**

While punctuality is about being on time, reliability is about being dependable in all aspects of your work. Here's how to boost your reliability:

## 1. Under-promise and Over-deliver

Always give yourself a little wiggle room when making commitments. If you think you can finish a project in a week, promise it in 10 days. Then, surprise and delight by delivering early.

## 2. Communicate Proactively

If you're going to be late or miss a deadline (hey, life happens), communicate as early as possible. Offer solutions, not just explanations.

## 3. Be Consistent

Reliability is about consistency. As author James Clear notes in his book "Atomic Habits," "You do not rise to the level of your goals. You fall to the level of your systems" [4]. Develop systems and habits that support your punctuality and reliability.

## 4. Take Responsibility

When things go wrong (and they sometimes will), own up to it. Don't make excuses or blame others. This level of accountability builds trust and respect.

### Case Study: The Japanese Railway System

Let's look at a real-world example of punctuality and reliability in action: the Japanese railway system. Japanese trains are famous for their punctuality, with an average delay of just 0.9 minutes [5].

How do they achieve this level of reliability? Through a combination of:

1. Meticulous planning and scheduling
2. Regular maintenance to prevent breakdowns
3. A culture that values punctuality and collective responsibility
4. Continuous improvement (they investigate and learn from every delay)

While we might not all be running railway systems, we can apply these principles to our own lives and work.

## The Ripple Effect of Punctuality and Reliability

When you become known as someone who's always on time and always delivers, you create a positive ripple effect:

1. **Trust**: People learn they can count on you, which often leads to more responsibilities and opportunities.

2. **Respect**: Your punctuality and reliability show respect for others, which is often reciprocated.

3. **Reduced Stress**: When you're not constantly rushing or scrambling to meet deadlines, your stress levels decrease.

4. **Improved Relationships**: Punctuality and reliability are cornerstones of strong professional (and personal) relationships.

## Overcoming Challenges

Of course, being punctual and reliable isn't always easy. You might face unexpected obstacles, competing priorities, or ingrained habits. Here are a few strategies for overcoming these challenges:

1. **Start Small**: If you're chronically late, start by aiming to be on time for one important event each day. Gradually increase from there.

2. **Identify Your Time Thieves**: Track your time for a week to identify what's causing delays. Is it social media? Underestimating travel time? Once you know, you can address it.

3. **Create Accountability**: Share your punctuality goals with a colleague or friend. Ask them to check in on your progress.

4. **Reframe Your Thinking**: Instead of seeing punctuality as a burden, view it as a way of valuing yourself and others.

Conclusion

Being punctual and reliable might not seem as exciting as some other career strategies, but it's a powerful way to stand out and get ahead. It's about more than just showing up on time – it's about showing up as your best self, ready to deliver on your promises.

Remember, as author Charles Marshall once said in essence, "Integrity is doing the right thing, even when no one is watching" [6]. Punctuality and reliability are forms of integrity that will serve you well throughout your career and life.

So set that alarm, make that commitment, and show up ready to conquer. Your future success will thank you for it!

---

References:

[1] Salary.com. (2014). Wasted Time at Work Costing Companies Billions.

[2] Franklin, B. (1748). Advice to a Young Tradesman.

[3] Kahneman, D., & Tversky, A. (1979). Intuitive prediction: Biases and corrective procedures. TIMS Studies in Management Science, 12, 313-327.

[4] Clear, J. (2018). Atomic Habits: An Easy & Proven Way to Build Good Habits & Break Bad Ones. Penguin Random House.

[5] Central Japan Railway Company. (2016). Data Book 2016.

[6] paraphrase of a Charles Marshall quote in *Shattering the Glass Slipper*. Prominent Publishing 2003.

# Chapter 4: Practice Active Listening and Empathy

In a world where everyone seems to be shouting to be heard, the ability to truly listen and empathize is like having a superpower. It's not just about being nice (although that's a bonus); it's about being effective, building strong relationships, and yes, standing out from the crowd.

## The Power of Active Listening and Empathy

Imagine you're at a party. There are two types of people: those who talk endlessly about themselves, and those who ask questions and genuinely listen to the answers. Which one do you think people remember fondly? That's right, the listeners.

The same principle applies in the professional world. When you practice active listening and empathy, you're not just hearing words; you're understanding contexts, picking up on subtle cues, and connecting on a deeper level. It's like having X-ray vision for communication.

## What is Active Listening?

Active listening is not just about staying quiet while someone else talks. It's an engaged, intentional form of listening that involves:

1. Giving your full attention to the speaker
2. Showing that you're listening through verbal and non-verbal cues
3. Providing feedback
4. Deferring judgment
5. Responding appropriately

As author Stephen R. Covey puts it in his book "The 7 Habits of Highly Effective People": "Most people do not listen with the intent to understand; they listen with the intent to reply" [1]. Active listening flips this script.

## The Empathy Factor

Empathy takes listening to the next level. It's about putting yourself in the other person's shoes, understanding their feelings and perspectives. As Brené Brown, renowned researcher and author, defines it: "Empathy is feeling with people" [2].

# Strategies for Active Listening

Let's dive into some practical strategies to boost your active listening skills:

## 1. The HEAR Technique

Use the HEAR acronym as a guide:
- Halt: Stop whatever else you're doing
- Engage: Give your full attention
- Anticipate: Look forward to what the person has to say
- Replay: Reflect on what you've heard

## 2. Use Non-Verbal Cues

Maintain eye contact, nod when appropriate, and use facial expressions to show you're engaged. A study by Albert Mehrabian found that 55% of communication is non-verbal [3], so these cues matter!

## 3. Ask Clarifying Questions

Don't assume you understand everything. Ask questions like, "What I'm hearing is... Is that correct?" This shows you're engaged and helps prevent misunderstandings.

## 4. Avoid Interrupting

It can be tempting to jump in with your own thoughts, but resist the urge. As author Simon Sinek says, "There is a difference between listening and waiting for your turn to speak" [4].

## 5. Summarize and Reflect

At appropriate intervals, summarize what you've heard. This confirms your understanding and shows you've been paying attention.

## Cultivating Empathy

Now, let's look at how to develop your empathy muscles:

## 1. Practice Perspective-Taking

Actively try to see situations from others' points of view. This doesn't mean you have to agree, just understand.

## 2. Be Curious About Others

Ask questions about people's experiences and feelings.
Genuine curiosity is the foundation of empathy.

## 3. Acknowledge Emotions

Recognize and validate others' emotions. A simple "That must
be tough" can go a long way.

## 4. Read Fiction

Yes, really! Studies have shown that reading literary fiction
can improve empathy [5]. So, that novel on your nightstand?
It's professional development!

## 5. Practice Mindfulness

Mindfulness can help you stay present and attuned to others.
Even a few minutes of daily meditation can make a difference.

## Case Study: Satya Nadella's Empathetic Leadership at Microsoft

When Satya Nadella took over as CEO of Microsoft in 2014, he brought a new leadership style focused on empathy and listening. In his book "Hit Refresh," Nadella writes about the importance of "empathy in innovation" [6].

Under Nadella's leadership, Microsoft shifted from a competitive, siloed culture to one of collaboration and growth mindset. The result? Microsoft's stock price tripled, and it became one of the world's most valuable companies.

Nadella's approach shows how active listening and empathy can transform not just individual relationships, but entire organizations.

## The Ripple Effect of Listening and Empathy

When you become known as someone who truly listens and empathizes, you create a positive ripple effect:

1. **Trust**: People feel comfortable sharing ideas and concerns with you.

2. **Innovation**: By understanding others' perspectives, you can identify new opportunities and solutions.

3. **Conflict Resolution**: Active listening and empathy are key skills in resolving conflicts effectively.

4. **Leadership**: These skills are crucial for effective leadership. As Richard Branson says, "Listen more than you talk. Nobody learned anything by hearing themselves speak" [7].

## Overcoming Challenges

Developing active listening and empathy skills isn't always easy. Here are some common challenges and how to overcome them:

1. **Distractions**: In our hyper-connected world, distractions are everywhere. Practice being fully present in conversations, even if it means putting your phone away.

2. **Assumptions**: We often think we know what someone's going to say. Challenge your assumptions and listen with an open mind.

3. **Emotional Reactions**: Sometimes, what we hear triggers emotional reactions. Practice pausing before responding to give yourself time to process.

4. **Time Pressure**: In a fast-paced work environment, it can feel like there's no time for deep listening. Remember that the time invested in listening often saves time in the long run by preventing misunderstandings.

## Conclusion

Active listening and empathy might not be the flashiest skills in your professional toolkit, but they're among the most powerful. They're the secret sauce that can transform your relationships, boost your effectiveness, and yes, help you stand out from the crowd.

Remember, as motivational speaker Roy T. Bennett said, "Listen with curiosity. Speak with honesty. Act with integrity" [8]. By cultivating these skills, you're not just improving your professional prospects; you're becoming a better colleague, leader, and human being.

So, in your next conversation, try turning down the volume on your internal monologue and tuning in to the person in front of you. You might be surprised at what you hear – and where it leads you.

---

References:

[1] Covey, S. R. (1989). The 7 Habits of Highly Effective People. Free Press.

[2] Brown, B. (2013). Empathy vs Sympathy. RSA Short.

[3] Mehrabian, A. (1980). Silent Messages: Implicit Communication of Emotions and Attitudes. Wadsworth.

[4] Sinek, S. (2011). Start with Why: How Great Leaders Inspire Everyone to Take Action. Portfolio.

[5] Kidd, D. C., & Castano, E. (2013). Reading Literary Fiction Improves Theory of Mind. Science, 342(6156), 377-380.

[6] Nadella, S. (2017). Hit Refresh: The Quest to Rediscover Microsoft's Soul and Imagine a Better Future for Everyone. Harper Business.

[7] Branson, R. (2014). The Virgin Way: Everything I Know About Leadership. Portfolio.

[8] Bennett, R. T. (2016). The Light in the Heart. Roy Bennett.

# Chapter 5: Maintain a Professional Online Presence

In today's digital age, your online presence is often the first impression you make. It's like your 24/7 business card, resume, and billboard all rolled into one. Whether you're job hunting, building a business, or simply aiming to stand out in your field, a professional online presence is no longer optional – it's essential.

## The Power of a Professional Online Presence

Think about the last time you met someone new in a professional context. Did you Google them afterward? Of course you did! We all do it. In fact, a study by CareerBuilder found that 70% of employers use social media to screen candidates during the hiring process [1]. Your online presence is your digital first impression, and as the saying goes, you never get a second chance to make a first impression.

## What Constitutes a Professional Online Presence?

A professional online presence isn't just about having a LinkedIn profile (although that's a great start). It's about strategically managing your digital footprint across various platforms. This includes:

1. Professional networking sites (e.g., LinkedIn)
2. Personal website or portfolio
3. Professional social media accounts
4. Industry-specific platforms or forums
5. Content you've created (articles, videos, podcasts, etc.)

**Strategies for Building Your Professional Online Presence**

Let's dive into some practical strategies to help you shine in the digital world:

1. Craft a Compelling LinkedIn Profile

LinkedIn is the go-to platform for professional networking. Here's how to make your profile stand out:

- Use a professional headshot: Profiles with professional photos get 14 times more views [2].
- Write a compelling headline: Don't just list your job title. Use this space to highlight your unique value proposition.

- Craft an engaging summary: Tell your professional story in a way that showcases your personality and achievements.
- Highlight key skills and get endorsements: This adds credibility to your profile.
- Regularly share relevant content: This keeps your profile active and demonstrates your industry knowledge.

## 2. Create a Personal Website or Portfolio

A personal website gives you complete control over your online narrative. It's like having your own piece of digital real estate. Use it to:

- Showcase your work and achievements
- Share your thoughts through a blog
- Provide a central hub for all your online activities

Remember, your website doesn't need to be complex. As Steve Krug says in his book "Don't Make Me Think," the key is to make your site intuitive and easy to navigate [3].

## 3. Leverage Social Media Strategically

Different social media platforms serve different purposes. Use them wisely:

- Twitter: Great for sharing quick insights and engaging in industry conversations.
- Instagram: Ideal if your work has a visual component.
- Facebook: Can be useful for certain industries, but be mindful of privacy settings.

Remember, it's better to be active on one or two platforms than to spread yourself too thin.

## 4. Create and Share Valuable Content

Content creation is a powerful way to demonstrate your expertise and add value to your network. This could include:

- Writing articles on LinkedIn or Medium
- Starting a blog on your website
- Creating videos or podcasts

As content marketing expert Ann Handley advises in her book "Everybody Writes," focus on creating content that is useful to your audience [4].

## 5. Engage in Online Communities

Participate in industry-specific forums, LinkedIn groups, or Twitter chats. This helps you:

- Stay up-to-date with industry trends
- Network with peers and potential mentors
- Showcase your knowledge by answering questions

**Case Study: Gary Vaynerchuk's Online Presence**

Let's look at a master of online presence: Gary Vaynerchuk. Gary V, as he's known, has built a massive following and multiple successful businesses largely through his strategic use of social media and content creation.

Key elements of Gary V's approach:

1. Consistent content creation across multiple platforms
2. Authenticity in his communication
3. Engagement with his audience
4. Adaptation to new platforms and trends

While you don't need to aim for Gary V's level of online fame, his strategies of consistency, authenticity, and engagement are valuable for anyone looking to build a strong online presence [5].

## The Benefits of a Strong Online Presence

Investing time in your online presence can pay off in numerous ways:

1. **Increased Visibility**: You become easier to find for potential employers, clients, or collaborators.
2. **Demonstrated Expertise**: Your online content showcases your knowledge and skills.
3. **Networking Opportunities**: A strong online presence can lead to valuable connections.
4. **Career Opportunities**: Many jobs are found through online networking.
5. **Personal Branding**: You control the narrative about your professional identity.

## Overcoming Common Challenges

Building and maintaining a professional online presence isn't without its challenges. Here's how to overcome some common ones:

1. **Time Management**: Start small. Even 15 minutes a day can make a difference. Use tools like Hootsuite or Buffer to schedule posts.

2. **Privacy Concerns**: Be mindful of what you share. As Jeff Bezos says, "Your brand is what people say about you when you're not in the room" [6]. Make sure your online presence reflects how you want to be perceived.

3. **Consistency**: Create a content calendar to help you stay consistent. Remember, it's a marathon, not a sprint.

4. **Writer's Block**: Not sure what to post? Share interesting articles, comment on industry news, or give a behind-the-scenes look at your work.

5. **Negative Feedback**: It's inevitable that not everyone will agree with you online. Handle criticism professionally and use it as an opportunity to engage in meaningful dialogue.

Conclusion

In the digital age, your online presence is an essential part of your professional identity. It's not about creating a perfect, polished image – it's about authentically showcasing your skills, knowledge, and personality in a way that resonates with your professional goals.

Remember, as Seth Godin says, "Marketing is no longer about the stuff that you make, but about the stories you tell" [7]. Your online presence is your opportunity to tell your professional story. Make it compelling!

So, update that LinkedIn profile, start that blog you've been thinking about, or share your insights on Twitter. Your future self (and your career) will thank you for it!

---

References:

[1] CareerBuilder. (2018). More Than Half of Employers Have Found Content on Social Media That Caused Them NOT to Hire a Candidate, According to Recent CareerBuilder Survey.

[2] LinkedIn. (2021). 20 steps to a better LinkedIn profile in 2021.

[3] Krug, S. (2013). Don't Make Me Think, Revisited: A Common Sense Approach to Web Usability. New Riders.

[4] Handley, A. (2014). Everybody Writes: Your Go-To Guide to Creating Ridiculously Good Content. Wiley.

[5] Vaynerchuk, G. (2018). Crushing It!: How Great Entrepreneurs Build Their Business and Influence-and How You Can, Too. Harper Business.

[6] Bezos, J. (attributed). Various sources.

[7] Godin, S. (2014). All Marketers are Liars: The Underground Classic That Explains How Marketing Really Works--and Why Authenticity Is the Best Marketing of All. Portfolio.

# Chapter 6: Volunteer for Challenging Projects

Picture this: You're at work, and suddenly, there's a buzz around the office. A new, high-profile project has just been announced. It's complex, it's challenging, and it's got 'career-defining opportunity' written all over it. While others hesitate, you step forward and volunteer. Congratulations! You've just taken a significant step towards standing out from the crowd.

## The Power of Volunteering for Challenges

Volunteering for challenging projects is like hitting the nitro boost in your career. It's not always easy, but it's almost always worth it. As management guru Peter Drucker once said, "The best way to predict the future is to create it" [1]. By taking on challenging projects, you're actively creating your future, shaping your career path, and distinguishing yourself from your peers.

## Why Challenging Projects Matter

Challenging projects are career gold for several reasons:

1. **Skill Development**: They push you out of your comfort zone and force you to learn new skills.
2. **Visibility**: They often put you in the spotlight, increasing your visibility within the organization.
3. **Networking**: They typically involve working with different teams or departments, expanding your professional network.
4. **Problem-Solving**: They provide opportunities to showcase your problem-solving abilities.
5. **Leadership**: They often come with leadership opportunities, even if you're not in a formal leadership role.

## Strategies for Tackling Challenging Projects

Let's dive into some strategies to help you not just survive, but thrive when volunteering for challenging projects:

### 1. Choose Wisely

Not all challenging projects are created equal. Look for projects that:
- Align with your career goals
- Leverage your strengths while stretching your abilities
- Have high visibility within the organization
- Solve important problems for the company

As Steve Jobs once said, "I'm convinced that about half of what separates successful entrepreneurs from the non-successful ones is pure perseverance" [2]. Choose projects that ignite your passion and fuel your perseverance.

2. Prepare Thoroughly

Once you've volunteered, preparation is key:
- Research the project thoroughly
- Identify potential challenges and brainstorm solutions
- Seek advice from colleagues who have worked on similar projects
- Develop a preliminary project plan

Remember, "By failing to prepare, you are preparing to fail," as Benjamin Franklin wisely noted [3].

3. Manage Expectations

Clear communication about project scope, timelines, and potential challenges is crucial:
- Set realistic goals and timelines
- Regularly update stakeholders on progress
- Be honest about challenges and setbacks

As project management expert Scott Berkun advises in his book "Making Things Happen," "The true definition of a project manager is someone who believes that nine women can deliver a baby in one month" [4]. Don't fall into this trap – manage expectations realistically from the start.

## 4. Build a Strong Team

If the project involves leading a team:
- Choose team members with complementary skills
- Foster a collaborative environment
- Encourage open communication and idea-sharing

Remember Google's Project Aristotle findings: psychological safety is the most important factor in building effective teams [5].

## 5. Embrace Learning Opportunities

Challenging projects are goldmines of learning opportunities:
- Be open to new ideas and approaches
- Seek feedback regularly
- Reflect on lessons learned throughout the project

As Carol Dweck explains in her book "Mindset," adopting a growth mindset – the belief that abilities can be developed through dedication and hard work – is crucial for success in challenging situations [6].

## Case Study: Mary Barra's Challenging Project at GM

Let's look at a real-world example of how volunteering for a challenging project can propel a career. Mary Barra, the CEO of General Motors, attributes much of her success to volunteering for a challenging project early in her career.

In the 1990s, as a young manager, Barra volunteered to oversee the launch of a new internal communications system at GM's Hamtramck plant. The project was complex and faced significant resistance from workers. However, Barra's perseverance and innovative approach to engaging employees made the project a success.

This project not only showcased Barra's leadership and problem-solving skills but also significantly raised her profile within the company. It was a crucial stepping stone on her path to becoming GM's first female CEO [7].

## The Ripple Effect of Tackling Challenges

When you successfully complete a challenging project, you create a positive ripple effect in your career:

1. **Increased Confidence**: Each challenge you overcome boosts your self-confidence.
2. **Enhanced Reputation**: You become known as someone who can handle tough assignments.
3. **Career Advancement**: Successful projects often lead to promotions or new opportunities.
4. **Personal Growth**: You develop not just professional skills, but also personal qualities like resilience and adaptability.

## Overcoming Common Obstacles

Of course, challenging projects come with... well, challenges. Here's how to overcome some common obstacles:

1. **Fear of Failure**: Remember, failure is a stepping stone to success. As Thomas Edison said, "I have not failed. I've just found 10,000 ways that won't work" [8].

2. **Imposter Syndrome**: Remind yourself that you were chosen for this project for a reason. Your skills and potential are real.

3. **Overwhelm**: Break the project down into smaller, manageable tasks. Celebrate small wins along the way.

4. **Resistance from Others**: Use your active listening and empathy skills (remember Chapter 4?) to understand and address concerns.

5. **Resource Constraints**: Get creative. Sometimes constraints can fuel innovation.

## Conclusion

Volunteering for challenging projects is not for the faint of heart. It requires courage, perseverance, and a willingness to step out of your comfort zone. But the rewards – in terms of skill development, career advancement, and personal growth – are immeasurable.

Remember, as motivational speaker Les Brown says, "If you put yourself in a position where you have to stretch outside your comfort zone, then you are forced to expand your consciousness" [9]. Each challenging project you take on is an opportunity to expand your consciousness, your skills, and your career horizons.

So, the next time a challenging project comes up, take a deep breath, raise your hand, and volunteer. Your future self will thank you for it!

---

References:

[1] Drucker, P. F. (1993). The Ecological Vision: Reflections on the American Condition. Transaction Publishers.

[2] Jobs, S. (1995). Smithsonian Institution Oral and Video Histories: Steve Jobs. Smithsonian Institution.

[3] Franklin, B. (attributed). Various sources.

[4] Berkun, S. (2008). Making Things Happen: Mastering Project Management. O'Reilly Media.

[5] Duhigg, C. (2016). What Google Learned From Its Quest to Build the Perfect Team. The New York Times Magazine.

[6] Dweck, C. S. (2006). Mindset: The New Psychology of Success. Random House.

[7] Colby, L. (2015). Road to Power: How GM's Mary Barra Shattered the Glass Ceiling. Wiley.

[8] Edison, T. A. (attributed). Various sources.

[9] Brown, L. (attributed). Various sources.

# Chapter 7: Cultivate a Strong Personal Brand

Picture this: You walk into a supermarket, and you're faced with rows upon rows of cereal boxes. How do you choose? Chances are, you reach for a brand you know and trust. Now, imagine if you could create that same level of recognition and trust for yourself in your professional life. That's the power of a strong personal brand.

## The Power of Personal Branding

Personal branding isn't just for celebrities or social media influencers. In today's competitive professional landscape, it's a crucial tool for anyone looking to stand out and advance their career. As Amazon founder Jeff Bezos famously said, "Your brand is what other people say about you when you're not in the room" [1].

## What is a Personal Brand?

Your personal brand is the unique combination of skills, experiences, and personality that you want the world to see.

It's the telling of your story, and how it reflects your conduct, behavior, spoken and unspoken words, and attitudes [2].

**Strategies for Cultivating Your Personal Brand**

Let's dive into some practical strategies to help you build a personal brand that resonates and gets you noticed:

1. Define Your Unique Value Proposition

Start by asking yourself:
- What are my strengths?
- What makes me different from others in my field?
- What do I want to be known for?

As personal branding expert William Arruda suggests, "Your personal brand is your unique promise of value." It separates you from your peers, your colleagues, and your competitors [3].

2. Identify Your Target Audience

Your brand should speak to the people you want to influence. Consider:
- Who are the key stakeholders in your career?

- What industry or niche do you want to impact?
- Who can help you achieve your professional goals?

## 3. Craft Your Brand Story

Your brand story is the narrative that ties together your experiences, values, and aspirations. It should be:
- Authentic: True to who you are
- Consistent: Aligned across all platforms and interactions
- Memorable: Engaging and easy to recall

As author and entrepreneur Seth Godin puts it, "Marketing is no longer about the stuff that you make, but about the stories you tell" [4].

## 4. Develop Your Online Presence

In the digital age, your online presence is a crucial part of your personal brand. This includes:
- Your professional social media profiles (LinkedIn, Twitter, etc.)
- A personal website or blog
- Your contributions to online professional communities

Remember, as we discussed in Chapter 5, maintaining a professional online presence is key to standing out in today's digital world.

## 5. Network Strategically

Your network is an essential part of your personal brand. As you build relationships:
- Seek out mentors and sponsors
- Attend industry events and conferences
- Engage in professional organizations

Networking guru Keith Ferrazzi advises, "The currency of real networking is not greed but generosity" [5].

## 6. Deliver Consistent Value

Your personal brand is only as strong as the value you provide. Consistently deliver high-quality work and go above and beyond expectations. As discussed in Chapter 2, consistently delivering high-quality work is a powerful way to stand out.

## 7. Seek Visibility Opportunities

Look for opportunities to showcase your expertise:
- Speak at industry events
- Write articles or blog posts
- Volunteer for high-profile projects (as we discussed in Chapter 6)

## Case Study: Richard Branson's Personal Brand

Let's look at a master of personal branding: Richard Branson. The Virgin Group founder has built a powerful personal brand alongside his business empire. Key elements of Branson's personal brand include:

1. Authenticity: Branson is known for being himself, whether he's in a boardroom or on a kitesurfing adventure.
2. Innovation: His brand is synonymous with pushing boundaries and thinking differently.
3. Fun: Branson infuses a sense of fun and adventure into everything he does.
4. Visibility: He's not afraid to put himself out there, often literally, with publicity stunts and media appearances.

Branson's personal brand is so strong that it's become inextricably linked with the Virgin brand. As he says, "Branding demands commitment; commitment to continual re-invention;

striking chords with people to stir their emotions; and commitment to imagination. It is easy to be cynical about such things, much harder to be successful" [6].

## The Benefits of a Strong Personal Brand

Investing time in building your personal brand can pay off in numerous ways:

1. **Career Opportunities**: A strong personal brand can attract job offers, promotions, and business opportunities.
2. **Increased Credibility**: When your personal brand is well-established, people are more likely to trust your expertise.
3. **Higher Perceived Value**: A strong personal brand can command higher salaries or rates for your services.
4. **Expanded Network**: Your personal brand can attract like-minded professionals and mentors.
5. **Personal Fulfillment**: A personal brand aligned with your values can lead to greater career satisfaction.

## Overcoming Common Challenges

Building a personal brand isn't without its challenges. Here's how to overcome some common ones:

1. **Authenticity vs. Professionalism**: Strike a balance by being true to yourself while maintaining professional standards.

2. **Consistency**: Develop a personal brand style guide to help maintain consistency across all platforms.

3. **Time Management**: Start small. Even 15 minutes a day dedicated to your personal brand can make a difference.

4. **Fear of Self-Promotion**: Remember, it's not about bragging. It's about showcasing your value and helping others.

5. **Evolving Your Brand**: As you grow, your brand should evolve too. Regularly reassess and adjust your brand as needed.

## Conclusion

Cultivating a strong personal brand is not about creating a false image or bragging about your accomplishments. It's about authentically communicating your value, building meaningful relationships, and positioning yourself for success.

As personal branding pioneer Tom Peters says, "All of us need to understand the importance of branding. We are CEOs of our own companies: Me Inc. To be in business today, our most important job is to be head marketer for the brand called You" [7].

So, start thinking about your personal brand today. What do you want to be known for? What value do you bring? How can you authentically communicate that to the world? Your personal brand is your professional superpower – it's time to cultivate it and let it shine!

---

References:

[1] Bezos, J. (attributed). Various sources.

[2] Chritton, S. (2014). Personal Branding For Dummies. John Wiley & Sons.

[3] Arruda, W., & Dixson, K. (2007). Career Distinction: Stand Out by Building Your Brand. John Wiley & Sons.

[4] Godin, S. (2014). All Marketers are Liars: The Underground Classic That Explains How Marketing Really Works--and Why Authenticity Is the Best Marketing of All. Portfolio.

[5] Ferrazzi, K. (2005). Never Eat Alone: And Other Secrets to Success, One Relationship at a Time. Crown Business.

[6] Branson, R. (2011). Losing My Virginity: How I Survived, Had Fun, and Made a Fortune Doing Business My Way. Crown Business.

[7] Peters, T. (1997). The Brand Called You. Fast Company.

# Chapter 8: Network Strategically and Genuinely

Picture this: You're at a conference, surrounded by industry leaders and potential collaborators. Do you a) head straight for the buffet and hover there all evening, or b) take a deep breath, put on your friendliest smile, and start mingling? If you chose option b, congratulations! You're already on your way to mastering the art of strategic networking.

## The Power of Strategic Networking

Networking isn't just about collecting business cards or racking up LinkedIn connections. It's about building meaningful relationships that can propel your career forward. As the old saying goes, "It's not what you know, but who you know." But let's update that for the 21st century: "It's not just who you know, but how you cultivate and maintain those relationships."

## What is Strategic Networking?

Strategic networking is the art of building and nurturing professional relationships with purpose and authenticity. It's about creating a web of connections that can support your career goals, provide valuable insights, and open doors to new opportunities.

## Strategies for Effective Networking

Let's dive into some practical strategies to help you network like a pro:

### 1. Define Your Networking Goals

Before you start networking, ask yourself:
- What do I want to achieve through networking?
- Who are the key people or types of people I should connect with?
- What value can I offer to my network?

As networking expert Ivan Misner says, "The best way to approach networking is to think about what you can do for someone else, not what they can do for you" [1].

### 2. Cultivate a Networking Mindset

Approach networking with the right mindset:
- Be curious about others

- Look for ways to add value
- Think long-term rather than seeking immediate gains

Bestselling author Stephen R. Covey's teachings include the idea of "synergizing", which is the idea that working together with others can lead to better results than working alone" [2].

## 3. Perfect Your Elevator Pitch

Craft a concise, compelling introduction of yourself:
- Keep it under 30 seconds
- Highlight what makes you unique
- Tailor it to your audience

Practice your pitch until it feels natural. As communication expert Nancy Duarte says, "The most impactful presentations are those that effectively blend both analytical data and emotional appeals" [3].

## 4. Leverage Both Online and Offline Networking

In today's digital age, effective networking happens both online and offline:
- Attend industry events and conferences
- Join professional associations

- Engage in online communities and forums
- Use social media platforms strategically

Remember, as we discussed in Chapter 5, maintaining a professional online presence is crucial in modern networking.

## 5. Follow Up and Stay in Touch

Networking doesn't end when the event is over:
- Follow up with new contacts within 48 hours
- Connect on LinkedIn with a personalized message
- Share relevant articles or insights with your network
- Schedule regular check-ins with key contacts

As Keith Ferrazzi, author of "Never Eat Alone," advises, "The currency of real networking is not greed but generosity" [4].

## 6. Give Before You Get

Approach networking with a mindset of generosity:
- Offer help or resources without expecting anything in return
- Make introductions between people in your network
- Share your expertise freely

Adam Grant, in his book "Give and Take," shows that the most successful networkers are often the most generous [5].

## 7. Quality Over Quantity

Focus on building deep, meaningful relationships rather than collecting superficial connections:
- Invest time in nurturing key relationships
- Be selective about who you add to your network
- Prioritize quality interactions over quantity of contacts

**Case Study: Sheryl Sandberg's Networking Strategy**

Let's look at a master networker: Sheryl Sandberg, COO of Facebook (now Meta). Sandberg is known for her strategic and genuine approach to networking. Key elements of her strategy include:

1. Authenticity: Sandberg is known for being genuine in her interactions, sharing both successes and challenges.
2. Mentorship: She actively mentors others and credits her own mentors for her success.
3. Advocacy: Sandberg uses her network to advocate for causes she believes in, particularly women in leadership.

4. Value Creation: She consistently looks for ways to add value to her network, whether through introductions, advice, or opportunities.

Sandberg's approach to networking has not only advanced her own career but has also created a powerful platform for her to effect change in the tech industry and beyond [6].

## The Benefits of Strategic Networking

Investing time in strategic networking can yield numerous benefits:

1. **Career Opportunities**: Your network can alert you to job openings or business opportunities.
2. **Knowledge Sharing**: Networking exposes you to new ideas and perspectives.
3. **Increased Influence**: A strong network can amplify your voice and impact.
4. **Support System**: Your network can provide advice, mentorship, and emotional support.
5. **Personal Growth**: Networking challenges you to step out of your comfort zone and develop new skills.

## Overcoming Common Networking Challenges

Networking doesn't come naturally to everyone. Here's how to overcome some common challenges:

1. **Introversion**: Remember, networking isn't about being the loudest in the room. Active listening (remember Chapter 4?) is a powerful networking tool.

2. **Fear of Rejection**: Reframe networking as relationship-building. Not every interaction will lead to a lasting connection, and that's okay.

3. **Lack of Time**: Integrate networking into your daily routine. Share an interesting article on LinkedIn during your morning coffee, or schedule a quick virtual catch-up during lunch.

4. **Feeling Inauthentic**: If networking feels fake, you're doing it wrong. Focus on building genuine relationships based on mutual interest and respect.

5. **Not Knowing Where to Start**: Start with your existing connections. Reach out to old colleagues or classmates. Attend industry events or join professional associations in your field.

## Conclusion

Strategic and genuine networking is not about collecting business cards or gaining followers. It's about building a community of professional relationships that support your growth, offer diverse perspectives, and create mutual value.

As motivational speaker Jim Rohn famously said, "You are the average of the five people you spend the most time with" [7]. By networking strategically and genuinely, you're not just advancing your career – you're enriching your professional life and potentially changing the trajectory of your success.

So, the next time you're at a professional event, take a deep breath, put on that friendly smile, and start a conversation. Remember, everyone there is looking to connect – they're just waiting for someone like you to make the first move. Your next great opportunity, mentor, or friend might be just a "hello" away!

---

References:

[1] Misner, I. (2010). Networking Like a Pro: Turning Contacts into Connections. Entrepreneur Press.

[2] Covey, S. M.R. (2008). The Speed of Trust: The One Thing That Changes Everything. Free Press.

[3] Duarte, N. (2010). Resonate: Present Visual Stories that Transform Audiences. John Wiley & Sons.

[4] Ferrazzi, K. (2005). Never Eat Alone: And Other Secrets to Success, One Relationship at a Time. Crown Business.

[5] Grant, A. (2013). Give and Take: A Revolutionary Approach to Success. Viking.

[6] Sandberg, S. (2013). Lean In: Women, Work, and the Will to Lead. Knopf.

[7] Rohn, J. (attributed). Various sources.

# Chapter 9: Offer Creative Solutions to Problems

Picture this: You're in a meeting, and someone presents a problem that's been plaguing the team for weeks. While others nod in sympathy or rehash old ideas, you pipe up with a novel solution that makes everyone sit up and take notice. Congratulations! You've just demonstrated one of the most valuable skills in any professional setting: creative problem-solving.

## The Power of Creative Problem-Solving

In today's fast-paced, ever-changing business landscape, the ability to offer creative solutions to problems is more valuable than ever. It's not just about thinking outside the box; it's about reimagining the box altogether. As Albert Einstein famously said, "We cannot solve our problems with the same thinking we used when we created them" [1].

## What is Creative Problem-Solving?

Creative problem-solving is the process of redefining problems and opportunities, coming up with novel ideas, and then taking action on these new ideas. It's about approaching challenges with curiosity, openness, and a willingness to explore unconventional paths.

## Strategies for Offering Creative Solutions

Let's dive into some practical strategies to help you become a creative problem-solving maestro:

### 1. Reframe the Problem

Often, the key to finding a creative solution lies in how you frame the problem:
- Ask "Why?" multiple times to get to the root of the issue
- Look at the problem from different perspectives
- Challenge assumptions about the problem

As design thinking expert Tim Brown suggests, "Don't think of it as a problem. Think of it as a project" [2].

### 2. Encourage Divergent Thinking

Divergent thinking is all about generating multiple, diverse ideas:
- Use brainstorming techniques like mind mapping or SCAMPER
- Embrace wild ideas – they might lead to practical solutions
- Quantity over quality in the initial stages – aim for a high volume of ideas

Alex Osborn, the father of brainstorming, advises, "It is easier to tone down a wild idea than to think up a new one" [3].

## 3. Combine Ideas

Some of the most innovative solutions come from combining existing ideas in new ways:
- Look for connections between seemingly unrelated concepts
- Mix and match elements from different solutions
- Use analogies from other fields or industries

As Steve Jobs said, "Creativity is just connecting things" [4].

## 4. Embrace Constraints

Constraints can actually fuel creativity:
- View limitations as opportunities for innovation

- Ask "What if?" questions to challenge perceived constraints
- Use constraints to focus your creative efforts

IDEO's David Kelley notes, constraints and deadlines are great for creativity [5].

## 5. Prototype and Iterate

Don't wait for the perfect solution – start with a rough idea and refine it:
- Create quick, low-fidelity prototypes to test ideas
- Gather feedback and iterate on your solutions
- Be willing to fail fast and learn from mistakes

As Facebook's famous motto goes, "Done is better than perfect" (6).

## 6. Cultivate a Creative Mindset

Creativity is a skill that can be developed:
- Stay curious and open to new experiences
- Practice mindfulness to enhance your awareness and perception
- Make time for play and exploration

Researcher Mihaly Csikszentmihalyi suggests, "Creativity is a central source of meaning in our lives" [7].

7. Collaborate and Cross-Pollinate

Great ideas often emerge from collaboration:
- Seek input from diverse perspectives
- Create an environment where all ideas are welcomed
- Encourage cross-functional collaboration

As design firm IDEO's Tom Kelley says, "Enlightened trial and error succeeds over the planning of lone genius" [8].

**Case Study: LEGO's Creative Comeback**

Let's look at a real-world example of creative problem-solving: LEGO's remarkable turnaround in the early 2000s.

In the late 1990s, LEGO was facing bankruptcy. Their creative solution? They went back to basics while simultaneously embracing innovation:

1. They refocused on their core product: the LEGO brick.
2. They leveraged customer insights, even inviting adult fans to help design new sets.

3. They expanded into new markets with products like LEGO Mindstorms, which combines traditional bricks with robotics.
4. They embraced digital platforms, creating successful video games and movies.

By creatively reimagining their product and business model, LEGO transformed from a company on the brink of collapse to one of the world's most valuable brands [9].

## The Benefits of Offering Creative Solutions

Becoming known as someone who offers creative solutions can have numerous benefits:

1. **Career Advancement**: Creative problem-solvers are valuable in any organization.
2. **Increased Engagement**: Tackling problems creatively can make work more enjoyable and fulfilling.
3. **Innovation Leadership**: You can drive innovation in your team or organization.
4. **Adaptability**: Creative problem-solving skills help you adapt to changing circumstances.
5. **Personal Brand Enhancement**: You'll be known as a go-to person for tough challenges.

## Overcoming Obstacles to Creative Problem-Solving

Of course, offering creative solutions isn't always easy. Here's how to overcome some common obstacles:

1. **Fear of Failure**: Remember, every "failed" idea is a step towards the right solution. As Thomas Edison said, "I have not failed. I've just found 10,000 ways that won't work" [10].

2. **Groupthink**: Encourage diverse viewpoints and create psychological safety for sharing unconventional ideas.

3. **Time Pressure**: While deadlines can spark creativity, extreme time pressure can stifle it. Try time-boxing your creative sessions.

4. **Lack of Resources**: Remember, constraints can fuel creativity. Some of the most innovative solutions come from resource-limited environments.

5. **"We've Always Done It This Way"**: Challenge the status quo. Ask why things are done a certain way and if there might be a better approach.

## Conclusion

Offering creative solutions to problems is not about having a "eureka" moment or being the smartest person in the room. It's about approaching challenges with curiosity, openness, and persistence. It's about being willing to explore, experiment, and sometimes fail in the pursuit of innovative solutions.

As George Bernard Shaw said, "Imagination is the beginning of creation. You imagine what you desire, you will what you imagine, and at last, you create what you will" [11].

So, the next time you're faced with a challenge, take a deep breath, let your imagination run wild, and don't be afraid to suggest that off-the-wall idea. Your creative solution might just be the breakthrough your team or organization needs. And remember, in the world of problem-solving, the only bad idea is the one left unspoken!

---

References:

[1] Einstein, A. (attributed). Various sources.

[2] Brown, T. (2019). Change by Design: How Design Thinking Transforms Organizations and Inspires Innovation. HarperBusiness.

[3] Osborn, A.F. (1953). Applied Imagination: Principles and Procedures of Creative Problem-Solving. Charles Scribner's Sons.

[4] Jobs, S. (1996). Wired Magazine Interview.

[5] Kelley, D. & Kelley, T. (2013). Creative Confidence: Unleashing the Creative Potential Within Us All. Crown Currency.

[6] Reportedly painted on the wall Facebook's Headquarters in 2010.

[7] Csikszentmihalyi, M. (1997). Creativity: Flow and the Psychology of Discovery and Invention. HarperCollins.

[8] Kelley, T. (2001). The Art of Innovation: Lessons in Creativity from IDEO, America's Leading Design Firm. Currency.

[9] Robertson, D. & Breen, B. (2013). Brick by Brick: How LEGO Rewrote the Rules of Innovation and Conquered the Global Toy Industry. Random House.

[10] Edison, T. (attributed). Various sources.

[11] Shaw, G.B. (1921). Back to Methuselah.

# Chapter 10: Write Articles or Create Content in Your Area of Expertise

Picture this: You're scrolling through your LinkedIn feed, and suddenly you see a colleague's name attached to a thought-provoking article. You click, you read, you're impressed. Suddenly, you're seeing this person in a whole new light. That, my friends, is the power of creating content in your area of expertise.

## The Power of Content Creation

In today's digital age, content is king. And when you create content in your area of expertise, you're not just sharing knowledge – you're positioning yourself as a thought leader, building your personal brand, and opening doors to new opportunities. As content marketing guru Ann Handley says, "In an online world, our online words are our emissaries; they tell the world who we are" [1].

## What Constitutes Expert Content?

Expert content can take many forms:
- Articles and blog posts
- Videos and podcasts
- Infographics and data visualizations
- Whitepapers and e-books
- Social media posts and threads

The key is that it provides value to your audience by sharing your unique insights and expertise.

## Strategies for Creating Compelling Content

Let's dive into some practical strategies to help you become a content creation maestro:

### 1. Know Your Audience

Before you start creating, ask yourself:
- Who am I writing for?
- What problems or questions do they have?
- How can my expertise help them?

As marketing expert Seth Godin advises, "Don't find customers for your products, find products for your customers" [2]. The same principle applies to content.

## 2. Choose Your Platform

Different types of content work better on different platforms:
- LinkedIn is great for professional articles
- Medium can help you reach a broader audience
- Your own blog gives you full control over your content
- YouTube is perfect for video content
- Twitter can be great for sharing quick insights or starting conversations

Choose the platform(s) where your target audience is most active.

## 3. Develop a Content Calendar

Consistency is key in content creation. A content calendar can help you:
- Plan your topics in advance
- Ensure a good mix of content types
- Stay consistent with your posting schedule

As social media expert Gary Vaynerchuk says, "Content is king, but context is God" [3]. A content calendar helps you provide the right content at the right time.

## 4. Focus on Quality Over Quantity

It's better to publish one high-quality piece per month than four mediocre ones:
- Take the time to research your topics thoroughly
- Back up your points with data and examples
- Edit and refine your work before publishing

Remember, as William Zinsser writes in "On Writing Well," "The secret of good writing is to strip every sentence to its cleanest components" [4].

## 5. Tell Stories

Humans are wired for storytelling. Incorporate anecdotes and case studies into your content to make it more engaging and memorable. As author Maya Angelou said, "People will forget what you said, people will forget what you did, but people will never forget how you made them feel" [5].

## 6. Engage with Your Audience

Content creation isn't a one-way street:
- Respond to comments on your articles
- Encourage discussion and debate
- Ask your audience what topics they'd like you to cover

Building this engagement can lead to a loyal following and even more content ideas.

7. Repurpose and Cross-Promote

Get more mileage out of your content by repurposing it for different platforms:
- Turn a long-form article into a series of social media posts
- Create an infographic summarizing your key points
- Expand on a popular social media post to create a full article

As content strategist Jay Baer says, "Content is fire, social media is gasoline" [6].

**Case Study: Neil Patel's Content Empire**

Let's look at a master of content creation: Neil Patel, digital marketing expert and entrepreneur.

Patel built his reputation and businesses largely through consistent, high-quality content creation:

1. He maintains an active blog, publishing in-depth articles on digital marketing topics.
2. He creates video content for YouTube, breaking down complex marketing concepts.
3. He's active on social media, sharing quick tips and engaging with his audience.
4. He offers free tools and resources, further establishing his expertise.

Patel's approach to content creation has not only positioned him as a thought leader in digital marketing but has also driven significant business success [7].

## The Benefits of Creating Expert Content

Consistently creating content in your area of expertise can yield numerous benefits:

1. **Establish Thought Leadership**: You position yourself as an expert in your field.
2. **Build Your Personal Brand**: Your content becomes part of your professional identity.

3. **Network Expansion**: Creating content can lead to new connections and opportunities.
4. **Career Advancement**: Demonstrating your expertise can open doors to new roles or clients.
5. **Continuous Learning**: The process of creating content deepens your own understanding.

## Overcoming Common Content Creation Challenges

Creating content consistently isn't always easy. Here's how to overcome some common challenges:

1. **Writer's Block**: Keep a running list of content ideas. Draw inspiration from questions you're asked at work or trending topics in your industry.

2. **Time Constraints**: Start small. Even a 300-word LinkedIn post once a week is a great start. As author Anne Lamott advises, take it "bird by bird" [8].

3. **Fear of Criticism**: Remember, not everyone will agree with you, and that's okay. Constructive debate can lead to even better content.

4. **Imposter Syndrome**: Remember, you don't need to know everything to share valuable insights. Your unique perspective is valuable.

5. **Measuring Impact**: Don't get discouraged if you don't see immediate results. Building an audience takes time. Focus on consistency and quality.

## Conclusion

Creating content in your area of expertise is not about showing off or proclaiming yourself as the ultimate authority. It's about sharing your knowledge, sparking conversations, and contributing to your professional community.

As marketing expert Jay Baer says, "If your stories are all about your products and services, that's not storytelling. It's a brochure. Give yourself permission to make the story bigger" [9].

So, open that blank document, fire up that camera, or start that podcast. Your unique insights and experiences are valuable, and there's an audience out there waiting to hear from you. Who knows? Your next article or video might just be the one that catapults you to the next level in your career. And remember, every expert was once a beginner – the key is to start creating and keep improving. Your future thought-leader self will thank you!

---

References:

[1] Handley, A. (2014). Everybody Writes: Your Go-To Guide to Creating Ridiculously Good Content. Wiley.

[2] Godin, S. (2009). Purple Cow: Transform Your Business by Being Remarkable. Portfolio.

[3] Vaynerchuk, G. (2013). Jab, Jab, Jab, Right Hook: How to Tell Your Story in a Noisy Social World. HarperBusiness.

[4] Zinsser, W. (2016). On Writing Well: The Classic Guide to Writing Nonfiction. Harper Perennial.

[5] Angelou, M. (attributed). Various sources.

[6] Baer, J. (2013). Youtility: Why Smart Marketing Is about Help Not Hype. Portfolio.

[7] Patel, N. (2021). "About Neil Patel". NeilPatel.com.

[8] Lamott, A. (1994). Bird by Bird: Some Instructions on Writing and Life. Anchor.

[9] Baer, J. (2013). Youtility: Why Smart Marketing Is about Help Not Hype. Portfolio.

# Chapter 11: Mentor Others in Your Field

Picture this: You're at the pinnacle of your career, looking back on your journey. What do you see? The projects you've completed? The promotions you've earned? Sure, those are great. But what if you also saw a trail of professionals you've guided, supported, and inspired along the way? That, my friends, is the power of mentoring.

## The Power of Mentoring

Mentoring others in your field isn't just a nice thing to do – it's a powerful strategy for standing out and advancing your own career. As leadership expert John C. Maxwell puts it, "One of the greatest values of mentors is the ability to see ahead what others cannot see and to help them navigate a course to their destination" [1].

## What is Mentoring?

At its core, mentoring is a relationship in which a more experienced or knowledgeable person guides a less experienced or knowledgeable person. But it's so much more than just giving advice. It's about:

- Sharing knowledge and experiences
- Providing guidance and support
- Challenging mentees to grow and develop
- Offering a different perspective
- Being a sounding board and cheerleader

## Strategies for Effective Mentoring

Let's dive into some practical strategies to help you become a mentoring maestro:

1. Be Clear About Expectations

Start your mentoring relationship on the right foot:
- Define the goals of the mentorship
- Agree on the frequency and method of communication
- Discuss confidentiality and boundaries

As mentoring expert Lois J. Zachary advises, clarity of expectations leads to productivity in the mentoring relationship [2].

## 2. Listen More Than You Speak

Effective mentoring isn't about having all the answers:
- Practice active listening (remember Chapter 4?)
- Ask thought-provoking questions
- Encourage your mentee to find their own solutions

Management guru Peter Drucker famously said, "The most important thing in communication is hearing what isn't said" [3].

## 3. Share Your Failures as Well as Your Successes

Your mentee can learn as much (if not more) from your mistakes as from your successes:
- Be honest about challenges you've faced
- Explain how you overcame obstacles
- Show that failure is a normal part of professional growth

As author J.K. Rowling said in her Harvard commencement speech, "It is impossible to live without failing at something, unless you live so cautiously that you might as well not have lived at all" [4].

## 4. Provide Constructive Feedback

Feedback is crucial for growth, but it needs to be delivered effectively:
- Be specific and actionable in your feedback
- Focus on behavior, not personality
- Balance positive feedback with areas for improvement

Remember the sandwich method: positive feedback, area for improvement, positive feedback.

## 5. Lead by Example

Your mentee will learn as much from what you do as what you say:
- Demonstrate the professional behaviors you want to see
- Show how to balance work and life
- Exhibit ethical decision-making

As Albert Einstein said, "Setting an example is not the main means of influencing others; it is the only means" [5].

## 6. Connect Your Mentee with Your Network

One of the most valuable things you can offer as a mentor is access to your professional network:

- Make introductions to key people in your field
- Recommend your mentee for opportunities when appropriate
- Teach networking skills by example

Remember, your network is one of your most valuable professional assets. Sharing it can be a powerful way to support your mentee.

## 7. Encourage Independence

The goal of mentoring is to help your mentee grow, not to create dependency:
- Gradually reduce the level of support as your mentee develops
- Encourage your mentee to seek multiple perspectives, not just yours
- Celebrate when your mentee outgrows the need for your mentorship

As Richard Branson says, "Train people well enough so they can leave, treat them well enough so they don't want to" [6].

**Case Study: Oprah Winfrey's Mentoring Legacy**

Let's look at a master mentor: Oprah Winfrey. Throughout her career, Oprah has been known for mentoring and supporting others, particularly women and people of color in the media industry.

Some key aspects of Oprah's mentoring approach:

1. She shares her own experiences openly, including her struggles and failures.
2. She provides opportunities for growth, often featuring protégés on her shows and in her productions.
3. She offers both personal and professional guidance, recognizing that the two are often intertwined.
4. She maintains long-term relationships with mentees, supporting their growth over many years.

Oprah's commitment to mentoring has not only helped numerous individuals in their careers but has also enhanced her own reputation as a leader and influencer in the media industry.

## The Benefits of Mentoring Others

Mentoring isn't just beneficial for the mentee. As a mentor, you can:

1. **Enhance Your Leadership Skills**: Mentoring helps you develop crucial leadership skills like communication, empathy, and motivation.
2. **Gain Fresh Perspectives**: Your mentees can offer new insights and ideas, keeping you connected to emerging trends in your field.
3. **Build Your Network**: Mentoring expands your professional network and can lead to new opportunities.
4. **Boost Your Reputation**: Being known as a mentor enhances your professional reputation and personal brand.
5. **Experience Personal Fulfillment**: There's a unique satisfaction in helping others grow and succeed.

## Overcoming Common Mentoring Challenges

Mentoring, while rewarding, isn't without its challenges. Here's how to overcome some common ones:

1. **Time Management**: Set clear boundaries and stick to scheduled mentoring sessions. Quality is more important than quantity.

2. **Difficult Conversations**: Be honest but kind when you need to give tough feedback. Remember, growth often happens outside the comfort zone.

3. **Generational Differences**: Be open to learning from your mentee, especially about new technologies or trends. Mentoring can be a two-way street.

4. **Maintaining Boundaries**: Be clear about what you can and can't offer. It's okay to say no to requests that cross professional boundaries.

5. **Measuring Progress**: Regularly review goals and celebrate milestones, both big and small, to track progress and maintain motivation.

## Conclusion

Mentoring others in your field is more than just a nice-to-have in your professional toolkit – it's a powerful strategy for standing out, growing your own skills, and leaving a lasting impact on your industry.

As Maya Angelou beautifully put it, "In order to be a mentor, and an effective one, one must care. You must care. You don't have to know how many square miles are in Idaho, you don't need to know what is the chemical makeup of chemistry, or of blood or water. Know what you know and care about the person, care about what you know and care about the person you're sharing with" [7].

So, take a look around. Is there someone in your field who could benefit from your experience and guidance? Reach out, offer your support, and start your mentoring journey. Not only will you be helping someone else grow, but you'll also be investing in your own growth and success. Remember, in the world of mentoring, the more you give, the more you gain!

---

References:

[1] Maxwell, J. C. (2008). Mentoring 101: What Every Leader Needs to Know. Harper Collins Leadership.

[2] Zachary, L. J. (2016). The Mentor's Guide: Facilitating Effective Learning Relationships. Jossey-Bass.

[3] Drucker, P. F. (2001). Management Challenges for the 21st Century. HarperBusiness.

[4] Rowling, J.K. (2008). Harvard Commencement Speech.

[5] Einstein, A. (attributed). Various sources.

[6] Branson, R. (2014). The Virgin Way: Everything I Know About Leadership. Portfolio.

[7] Angelou, M. (2013). Interview with George Stroumboulopoulos, CBC.

# Chapter 12: Continuously Educate Yourself and Stay Updated

Picture this: You're in a meeting, and someone mentions a cutting-edge technology that's revolutionizing your industry. While others scratch their heads, you nod knowingly, ready to contribute to the discussion. That, my friends, is the power of continuous learning and staying updated.

## The Power of Lifelong Learning

In today's fast-paced, ever-changing world, the ability to continuously learn and adapt is not just an asset—it's a necessity. As Alvin Toffler, the famous futurist, once said, "The illiterate of the 21st century will not be those who cannot read and write, but those who cannot learn, unlearn, and relearn" [1].

## What is Continuous Education?

Continuous education goes beyond formal degrees or certifications. It's about:

- Staying current with industry trends and developments
- Expanding your skill set
- Deepening your expertise in your field
- Exploring adjacent disciplines
- Developing a growth mindset

## Strategies for Continuous Learning

Let's dive into some practical strategies to help you become a lifelong learning maestro:

### 1. Set Learning Goals

Just like any other aspect of your career, learning should be purposeful:
- Identify skills or knowledge areas you want to develop
- Set SMART (Specific, Measurable, Achievable, Relevant, Time-bound) learning goals
- Review and adjust your goals regularly

As Peter Drucker, the management guru, advises, "What gets measured gets managed" [2].

## 2. Embrace Online Learning

The internet has democratized education. Take advantage of:
- Massive Open Online Courses (MOOCs) from platforms like Coursera, edX, or Udacity
- Webinars and virtual conferences
- YouTube tutorials and educational channels
- Podcasts in your field of interest

Remember, as the ancient Chinese proverb goes, "Learning is a treasure that will follow its owner everywhere" [3].

## 3. Read Voraciously

Reading is one of the most efficient ways to gain new knowledge:
- Set a reading goal (e.g., one book per month)
- Follow industry blogs and publications
- Subscribe to relevant newsletters
- Use apps like Blinkist for book summaries if you're short on time

Warren Buffett, when asked about the key to success, said, "Read 500 pages like this every day. That's how knowledge works. It builds up, like compound interest" [4].

## 4. Attend Conferences and Workshops

In-person events offer unique learning and networking opportunities:
- Attend industry conferences
- Participate in workshops and seminars
- Consider presenting at these events to reinforce your learning

As motivational speaker Jim Rohn said, "Formal education will make you a living; self-education will make you a fortune" [5].

## 5. Learn from Your Network

Your professional network can be a valuable source of learning:
- Engage in discussions with colleagues and mentors
- Join professional associations in your field
- Participate in online forums and communities

Remember, "If you're the smartest person in the room, you're in the wrong room" [6].

6. Practice Reflection and Application

Learning isn't just about consuming information—it's about applying it:
- Keep a learning journal to reflect on what you've learned
- Look for opportunities to apply new knowledge in your work
- Share your learnings with others (remember Chapter 10 on creating content?)

As Confucius said, "I hear and I forget. I see and I remember. I do and I understand" [7].

7. Embrace Diverse Learning Methods

Everyone learns differently. Experiment with various methods:
- Visual (videos, infographics)
- Auditory (podcasts, audiobooks)
- Kinesthetic (hands-on projects, simulations)
- Social (group discussions, study groups)

Find what works best for you and lean into it.

## Case Study: Bill Gates' "Think Weeks"

Let's look at a master of continuous learning: Bill Gates. Throughout his career, Gates has been known for his voracious appetite for knowledge and his dedication to continuous learning.

One of Gates' most famous learning practices is his "Think Week." Twice a year, Gates would seclude himself for a week, armed with dozens of papers and books on various topics. During this time, he would read, reflect, and think deeply about technological trends and their implications for Microsoft and the world [8].

This practice not only kept Gates at the forefront of technological developments but also led to several strategic decisions for Microsoft, including the famous 1995 "Internet Tidal Wave" memo that redirected the company's focus towards the internet [9].

## The Benefits of Continuous Learning

Investing in continuous education can yield numerous benefits:

1. **Career Advancement**: Up-to-date skills and knowledge make you more valuable to employers.
2. **Adaptability**: You're better equipped to handle changes in your industry.
3. **Innovation**: New knowledge can spark creative ideas and solutions.
4. **Confidence**: The more you know, the more confident you become in your abilities.
5. **Personal Fulfillment**: Learning can be intrinsically rewarding and contribute to personal growth.

## Overcoming Common Learning Challenges

Continuous learning isn't always easy. Here's how to overcome some common challenges:

1. **Time Constraints**: Start small. Even 15 minutes a day can make a difference. Use "dead time" like commutes for learning.

2. **Information Overload**: Focus on quality over quantity. Use curation tools like Pocket or Feedly to manage information.

3. **Lack of Direction**: Refer back to your learning goals. If you're unsure, seek advice from mentors or colleagues.

4. **Motivation**: Connect your learning to your career goals. Celebrate small wins to stay motivated.

5. **Cost**: Remember, many high-quality learning resources are free or low-cost. Look for scholarships or employer support for more expensive options.

## Conclusion

Continuous education and staying updated isn't just about accumulating facts—it's about cultivating a mindset of curiosity and growth. It's about staying relevant, adaptable, and valuable in an ever-changing professional landscape.

As the famous UCLA basketball coach John Wooden said, "It's what you learn after you know it all that counts" [10].

So, pick up that book you've been meaning to read. Sign up for that online course. Attend that industry webinar. Your future self—more knowledgeable, more skilled, and more successful—will thank you for it. Remember, in the game of professional development, the real winning move is to never stop learning!

---

References:

[1] Toffler, A. (1970). Future Shock. Random House.

[2] Drucker, P. F. (1954). The Practice of Management. Harper & Row.

[3] Unknown. (Ancient Chinese Proverb).

[4] Buffett, W. (2007). University of Florida Speech.

[5] Rohn, J. (attributed). Various sources.

[6] Unknown. (Common saying in business circles).

[7] Confucius. (attributed). Various sources.

[8] Guth, R. A. (2005). "In Secret Hideaway, Bill Gates Ponders Microsoft's Future." The Wall Street Journal.

[9] Gates, B. (1995). "The Internet Tidal Wave." Internal Microsoft memo.

[10] Wooden, J. (2005). Wooden on Leadership. McGraw-Hill.

# Chapter 13: Develop Strong Public Speaking Skills

Picture this: You're standing in front of a room full of colleagues, all eyes on you. Your palms are sweaty, your heart is racing, but as you begin to speak, your voice is clear and confident. The audience is captivated. Congratulations! You've just harnessed one of the most powerful tools for standing out in your career: strong public speaking skills.

## The Power of Public Speaking

Public speaking is often cited as one of the most common fears, even outranking the fear of death for many people. Yet, it's also one of the most valuable skills you can develop in your professional life. As Warren Buffett once said, you can improve your value by 50 percent just by learning communication skills--public speaking  [1].

## What Constitutes Strong Public Speaking?

Strong public speaking goes beyond just delivering a message without fainting. It's about:

- Engaging your audience effectively
- Conveying your ideas clearly and persuasively
- Projecting confidence and authority
- Adapting to your audience's reactions
- Using verbal and non-verbal communication skillfully

**Strategies for Developing Strong Public Speaking Skills**

Let's dive into some practical strategies to help you become a public speaking maestro:

## 1. Know Your Audience

Before you even start preparing your content, understand who you'll be speaking to:
- What's their background?
- What do they care about?
- What do they already know about your topic?

As the ancient Greek philosopher Aristotle advised, "The fool tells me his reasons; the wise man persuades me with my own" [2].

## 2. Structure Your Speech

A well-structured speech is easier to deliver and understand:
- Start with a strong opening to grab attention
- Use the "rule of three" to organize your main points
- End with a memorable conclusion

Remember the old public speaking adage: "Tell them what you're going to tell them, tell them, then tell them what you told them" [3].

## 3. Practice, Practice, Practice

There's no substitute for practice:
- Rehearse your speech out loud, multiple times
- Use a mirror or record yourself to observe your delivery
- Practice in front of friends or family for feedback

As Malcolm Gladwell popularized in his book "Outliers," it often takes 10,000 hours of practice to achieve mastery in a field [4].

## 4. Master Non-Verbal Communication

Your body language speaks volumes:
- Maintain eye contact with your audience

- Use purposeful gestures to emphasize points
- Be aware of your facial expressions

According to Albert Mehrabian's often-cited study, 55% of communication is through body language, 38% through tone of voice, and only 7% through the actual words spoken [5].

## 5. Use Visual Aids Effectively

Visual aids can enhance your presentation, but use them judiciously:
- Keep slides simple and uncluttered
- Use images and graphics to illustrate points
- Don't read directly from your slides

As presentation guru Nancy Duarte says, "Slides should be a visual aid for the audience, not a visual aid for the speaker" [6].

## 6. Engage Your Audience

Turn your speech into a conversation:
- Ask rhetorical questions
- Use anecdotes and personal stories
- Incorporate audience participation when appropriate

Dale Carnegie, in his classic "How to Win Friends and Influence People," emphasized the importance of making others feel important and appreciated [7].

7. Handle Nerves Productively

Some nervousness is normal and can even be beneficial:
- Use deep breathing techniques to calm yourself
- Reframe nervousness as excitement
- Prepare thoroughly to boost your confidence

As Mark Twain supposedly quipped, "There are two types of speakers: those that are nervous and those that are liars" [8].

**Case Study: Steve Jobs' Stanford Commencement Speech**

Let's look at a master of public speaking: Steve Jobs. His 2005 Stanford commencement address is often cited as one of the greatest speeches of our time [9].

Key elements that made this speech powerful:

1. Structure: Jobs used three personal stories to illustrate his points, making the speech easy to follow and remember.

2. Authenticity: He shared personal, sometimes painful experiences, creating a strong connection with the audience.
3. Simplicity: His language was clear and concise, with no unnecessary jargon.
4. Powerful conclusion: He ended with the memorable phrase "Stay hungry, stay foolish," leaving the audience with a clear call to action.

This speech demonstrates how effective public speaking can create a lasting impact and enhance one's personal brand.

**The Benefits of Strong Public Speaking Skills**

Developing your public speaking skills can yield numerous benefits:

1. **Increased Visibility**: Good speakers often get more opportunities to represent their teams or organizations.
2. **Enhanced Leadership Perception**: Strong public speaking skills are often associated with leadership ability.
3. **Better Persuasion Skills**: Public speaking teaches you how to structure arguments and influence others.
4. **Improved Confidence**: As your speaking skills improve, so does your overall confidence.

5. **Networking Opportunities**: Speaking at events can help you connect with a wider professional network.

## Overcoming Common Public Speaking Challenges

Even seasoned speakers face challenges. Here's how to overcome some common ones:

1. **Stage Fright**: Remember, some nervousness is normal. Use it as energy to fuel your performance.

2. **Fear of Forgetting**: Use notes or cue cards as a safety net, but avoid reading directly from them.

3. **Difficult Questions**: It's okay to say "I don't know, but I'll find out" if you're unsure of an answer.

4. **Technical Difficulties**: Always have a backup plan. Be prepared to deliver your talk without slides if necessary.

5. **Tough Audience**: Focus on the engaged members of the audience. Their positive energy can be contagious.

## Conclusion

Developing strong public speaking skills is not about becoming the next TED Talk sensation overnight. It's about consistently working on your ability to communicate effectively, engage your audience, and convey your ideas with clarity and confidence.

As author Scott Berkun notes in his book "Confessions of a Public Speaker," "All speaking is public speaking, whether it's to one person or a thousand" [10]. So, whether you're presenting to your team, pitching to a client, or delivering a keynote at a conference, your public speaking skills are always on display.

Remember, every great speaker was once a nervous novice. The key is to start where you are, use what you have, and do what you can. Join a local Toastmasters club, volunteer to present at team meetings, or simply practice in front of your mirror. With each speech, you'll grow more confident, more skilled, and more likely to stand out in your professional life.

So, take a deep breath, step up to that podium (real or metaphorical), and let your voice be heard. Your future success may just depend on it!

---

References:

[1] Lowe, F. (2019). "Warren Buffett Says This Is the Most Valuable Skill You Can Have." Inc.com.

[2] Aristotle. (350 BCE). Rhetoric.

[3] Lucas, S. E. (2011). The Art of Public Speaking. McGraw-Hill Education.

[4] Gladwell, M. (2008). Outliers: The Story of Success. Little, Brown and Company.

[5] Mehrabian, A. (1971). Silent Messages. Wadsworth.

[6] Duarte, N. (2008). Slide:ology: The Art and Science of Creating Great Presentations. O'Reilly Media.

[7] Carnegie, D. (1936). How to Win Friends and Influence People. Simon & Schuster.

[8] Twain, M. (attributed). Various sources.

[9] Jobs, S. (2005). Stanford Commencement Address.

[10] Berkun, S. (2011). Confessions of a Public Speaker. O'Reilly Media.

# Chapter 14: Practice Exceptional Customer Service

Picture this: You're dealing with a company, and you have a problem. After being bounced around from department to department, you finally reach someone who not only solves your issue but does so with such genuine care and efficiency that you hang up the phone feeling like you've just made a new friend. That, my friends, is the power of exceptional customer service.

## The Power of Exceptional Customer Service

In today's competitive business landscape, exceptional customer service isn't just a nice-to-have—it's a must-have. As Maya Angelou famously said, "People will forget what you said, people will forget what you did, but people will never forget how you made them feel" [1]. This sentiment is at the heart of exceptional customer service.

## What Constitutes Exceptional Customer Service?

Exceptional customer service goes beyond just solving problems or answering questions. It's about:

- Anticipating customer needs
- Going above and beyond expectations
- Creating positive emotional experiences
- Building long-term relationships
- Turning customers into loyal advocates

## Strategies for Practicing Exceptional Customer Service

Let's dive into some practical strategies to help you become a customer service maestro:

### 1. Develop Empathy

Put yourself in your customer's shoes:
- Listen actively and attentively
- Try to understand the customer's perspective
- Show genuine care for their concerns

As author and customer service expert Shep Hyken teaches, there's a big difference between hearing and listening. Hearing is using your ears. Listening is using your brain [2].

## 2. Communicate Clearly and Positively

Your communication can make or break the customer experience:
- Use positive language even when delivering bad news
- Avoid technical jargon unless you're sure the customer understands it
- Be clear about what you can do, rather than what you can't

Remember the words of Stephen Covey: "Seek first to understand, then to be understood" [3].

## 3. Take Ownership

Don't pass the buck:
- If you can't solve the problem yourself, take responsibility for finding someone who can
- Follow up to ensure the issue has been resolved
- Learn from each interaction to improve future service

As Richard Branson, founder of Virgin Group, puts it, "The key is to set realistic customer expectations, and then not to just meet them, but to exceed them—preferably in unexpected and helpful ways" [4].

## 4. Personalize the Experience

Make each customer feel special:
- Use the customer's name
- Remember their preferences
- Tailor your solutions to their specific needs

According to a study by Accenture, 91% of consumers are more likely to shop with brands that recognize, remember, and provide them with relevant offers and recommendations [5].

## 5. Be Proactive

Don't wait for problems to arise:
- Anticipate potential issues and address them before they become problems
- Reach out to customers to ensure they're satisfied
- Offer helpful information or tips even when they haven't asked

As Bill Gates once said, "Your most unhappy customers are your greatest source of learning" [6].

## 6. Go the Extra Mile

Exceed expectations whenever possible:
- Offer solutions that go beyond what the customer asked for
- Follow up after the interaction to ensure continued satisfaction
- Look for opportunities to surprise and delight

Zappos, the online shoe retailer, is famous for its customer service. CEO Tony Hsieh once said, "We believe that customer service shouldn't be just a department; it should be the entire company" [7].

## 7. Continuously Improve

Use every interaction as a learning opportunity:
- Solicit feedback from customers
- Analyze customer service data to identify trends and areas for improvement
- Stay updated on industry best practices

As Peter Drucker, the father of modern management, said, "Quality in a service or product is not what you put into it. It is what the customer gets out of it" [8].

## Case Study: Ritz-Carlton's $2,000 Rule

Let's look at a master of customer service: The Ritz-Carlton Hotel Company. One of their most famous policies is the "$2,000 rule," which empowers every employee to spend up to $2,000 per incident to solve a customer's problem without needing to ask for a manager's permission.

This policy has led to numerous legendary stories of exceptional service. In one instance, when a guest left behind a laptop charger, a Ritz-Carlton employee not only mailed the charger to the guest but also included a power strip because the guest had mentioned needing more outlets in the room [9].

This approach demonstrates how empowering employees and prioritizing customer satisfaction can create memorable experiences and fierce brand loyalty.

### The Benefits of Practicing Exceptional Customer Service

Mastering the art of customer service can yield numerous benefits:

1. **Enhanced Reputation**: Word of mouth about great service can be your best marketing tool.
2. **Customer Loyalty**: Satisfied customers are more likely to return and recommend you to others.

3. **Career Advancement**: Customer service skills are valuable in almost any role or industry.
4. **Personal Satisfaction**: There's a unique joy in knowing you've made someone's day better.
5. **Conflict Resolution Skills**: These skills transfer well to other areas of your professional and personal life.

## Overcoming Common Customer Service Challenges

Even with the best intentions, customer service can be challenging. Here's how to overcome some common hurdles:

1. **Difficult Customers**: Stay calm and professional. Remember, their frustration is usually not personal.

2. **Limited Resources**: Be creative. Sometimes a sincere apology and explanation can go a long way.

3. **Burnout**: Practice self-care and set boundaries. You can't pour from an empty cup.

4. **Repetitive Questions**: Develop efficient systems or FAQs to handle common issues, freeing up time for more complex problems.

5. **Balancing Speed and Quality**: Strive for the right balance. Sometimes taking a little extra time leads to a much better resolution.

## Conclusion

Practicing exceptional customer service is not just about following a script or adhering to policies. It's about genuinely caring for the people you serve and consistently striving to create positive experiences.

As customer service expert Shep Hyken says, "Customer service is not a department. It's a philosophy to be embraced by every member of an organization, from the CEO to the most recently hired" [10].

Whether you're in a traditional customer service role or not, these skills are invaluable. Every interaction with colleagues, stakeholders, or actual customers is an opportunity to provide exceptional service. By consistently going above and beyond, you'll not only stand out in your current role but also pave the way for future success.

So, the next time you interact with someone in a professional capacity, ask yourself: "How can I make this experience exceptional?" Your commitment to service excellence might just be the differentiator that propels your career to new heights. Remember, in the world of customer service, every interaction is an opportunity to shine!

---

References:

[1] Angelou, M. (attributed). Various sources.

[2] Hyken, S. (2018). The Convenience Revolution: How to Deliver a Customer Service Experience that Disrupts the Competition and Creates Fierce Loyalty. Sound Wisdom.

[3] Covey, S. R. (1989). The 7 Habits of Highly Effective People. Free Press.

[4] Branson, R. (2014). The Virgin Way: Everything I Know About Leadership. Portfolio.

[5] Accenture. (2018). "Making it Personal: Pulse Check 2018."

[6] Gates, B. (1999). Business @ the Speed of Thought. Grand Central Publishing.

[7] Hsieh, T. (2010). Delivering Happiness: A Path to Profits, Passion, and Purpose. Grand Central Publishing.

[8] Drucker, P. F. (1985). Innovation and Entrepreneurship. Harper & Row.

[9] Solomon, M. (2016). The Heart of Hospitality: Great Hotel and Restaurant Leaders Share Their Secrets. Select Books.

[10] Hyken, S. (2011). The Amazement Revolution: Seven Customer Service Strategies to Create an Amazing Customer (and Employee) Experience. Greenleaf Book Group Press.

# Chapter 15: Cultivate a Growth Mindset and Adaptability

Picture this: You're faced with a challenging new project at work. Do you think, "I'm not sure I can do this," or do you think, "This is an opportunity to learn and grow"? If you chose the latter, congratulations! You're already on your way to cultivating a growth mindset and adaptability—two essential qualities for standing out and getting ahead in today's rapidly changing professional landscape.

## The Power of a Growth Mindset and Adaptability

In a world where the only constant is change, having a growth mindset and being adaptable isn't just beneficial—it's crucial for success. As Charles Darwin once said, "It is not the strongest of the species that survive, nor the most intelligent, but the one most responsive to change" [1]. This sentiment is just as true in the professional world as it is in nature.

## What are a Growth Mindset and Adaptability?

A growth mindset, a concept developed by psychologist Carol Dweck, is the belief that abilities and intelligence can be developed through effort, learning, and persistence [2]. Adaptability is the quality of being able to adjust to new conditions or changes in your environment.

Together, these qualities involve:

- Embracing challenges as opportunities for growth
- Persisting in the face of setbacks
- Seeing effort as a path to mastery
- Learning from criticism
- Finding inspiration in the success of others
- Being open to change and new ideas

**Strategies for Cultivating a Growth Mindset and Adaptability**

Let's dive into some practical strategies to help you become a growth mindset and adaptability maestro:

1. Embrace Challenges

Instead of avoiding difficult tasks, seek them out:
- Volunteer for projects outside your comfort zone
- Set stretch goals for yourself

- View challenges as opportunities to learn and grow

As author Ryan Holiday puts it, "The obstacle is the way" [3].

## 2. Reframe Failure

See failures not as defeats, but as learning experiences:
- Analyze what went wrong and how you can improve
- Share your learnings with others
- Celebrate the effort and lessons learned, not just the outcome

Thomas Edison famously said, "I have not failed. I've just found 10,000 ways that won't work" [4].

## 3. Cultivate Curiosity

Stay curious and open to new ideas:
- Ask questions and seek to understand different perspectives
- Read widely, both within and outside your field
- Attend workshops or conferences on new topics

Albert Einstein once said, "I have no special talent. I am only passionately curious" [5].

## 4. Practice Mindfulness

Being present and aware can help you adapt more easily to changes:
- Practice meditation or mindfulness exercises
- Take regular breaks to reflect on your thoughts and feelings
- Stay attuned to changes in your environment

Jon Kabat-Zinn, the creator of Mindfulness-Based Stress Reduction, advises, "You can't stop the waves, but you can learn to surf" [6].

## 5. Develop a Learning Orientation

See every experience as a chance to learn:
- Seek feedback regularly and act on it
- Keep a learning journal to reflect on your experiences
- Set aside time for deliberate learning and skill development

As Peter Senge writes in "The Fifth Discipline," "The only sustainable competitive advantage is an organization's ability to learn faster than the competition" [7].

## 6. Build Resilience

Resilience is key to maintaining a growth mindset in the face of adversity:
- Develop a strong support network
- Practice self-care and stress management techniques
- Focus on what you can control, and let go of what you can't

Psychologist Angela Duckworth, known for her work on grit, says, "Enthusiasm is common. Endurance is rare" [8].

## 7. Embrace Change

Instead of resisting change, learn to welcome it:
- Stay informed about trends in your industry
- Be proactive in adapting to new technologies or processes
- Look for opportunities in times of change

As management guru Peter Drucker said, "The greatest danger in times of turbulence is not the turbulence; it is to act with yesterday's logic" [9].

**Case Study: Satya Nadella's Transformation of Microsoft**

Let's look at a master of growth mindset and adaptability: Satya Nadella, CEO of Microsoft. When Nadella took over in

2014, Microsoft was struggling to adapt to the mobile and cloud computing era.

Nadella's approach exemplified a growth mindset and adaptability:

1. He shifted the company's focus from a "know-it-all" to a "learn-it-all" culture.
2. He embraced cloud computing, even though it initially threatened Microsoft's traditional software business.
3. He fostered partnerships with former rivals, showing adaptability in Microsoft's business strategy.
4. He encouraged experimentation and wasn't afraid to cut losses on unsuccessful projects.

Under Nadella's leadership, Microsoft's stock price tripled, and the company regained its position as a leader in the tech industry [10].

## The Benefits of a Growth Mindset and Adaptability

Cultivating these qualities can yield numerous benefits:

1. **Increased Resilience**: You'll bounce back faster from setbacks.

2. **Enhanced Learning**: You'll acquire new skills more readily.

3. **Improved Problem-Solving**: You'll approach challenges with more creativity and flexibility.

4. **Greater Career Opportunities**: You'll be better equipped to adapt to changing job markets.

5. **Reduced Stress**: You'll be less fazed by change and uncertainty.

## Overcoming Obstacles to Growth Mindset and Adaptability

Developing these qualities isn't always easy. Here's how to overcome some common challenges:

1. **Fixed Mindset Tendencies**: Catch yourself when you fall into fixed mindset thinking. Reframe your thoughts to align with a growth mindset.

2. **Fear of Failure**: Remember that failure is a natural part of learning and growth. As author Neil Gaiman said, "Make glorious, amazing mistakes" [11].

3. **Comfort Zone Attachment**: Regularly push yourself to try new things, even if they're small. Growth happens outside your comfort zone.

4. **Perfectionism**: Focus on progress, not perfection. Every step forward is a win.

5. **Negative Self-Talk**: Practice self-compassion. Treat yourself with the same kindness you'd offer a friend.

## Conclusion

Cultivating a growth mindset and adaptability isn't about becoming a different person overnight. It's about gradually shifting your perspective and habits to embrace learning, growth, and change.

As Carol Dweck herself says, "Becoming is better than being" [12]. By adopting a growth mindset and developing your adaptability, you're not just preparing for the future—you're actively shaping it.

So, the next time you face a challenge or a change, take a deep breath and ask yourself: "What can I learn from this? How can I grow?" Your willingness to embrace challenges and adapt to change might just be the key that unlocks the next level of your career.

Remember, in the grand game of professional development, those who learn to love the process of growth and change are the ones who truly stand out and get ahead. So go forth, grow, adapt, and watch as new opportunities unfold before you!

---

References:

[1] Darwin, C. (attributed). Various sources.

[2] Dweck, C. S. (2006). Mindset: The New Psychology of Success. Random House.

[3] Holiday, R. (2014). The Obstacle Is the Way: The Timeless Art of Turning Trials into Triumph. Portfolio.

[4] Edison, T. (attributed). Various sources.

[5] Einstein, A. (attributed). Various sources.

[6] Kabat-Zinn, J. (1994). Wherever You Go, There You Are: Mindfulness Meditation in Everyday Life. Hyperion.

[7] Senge, P. M. (1990). The Fifth Discipline: The Art & Practice of The Learning Organization. Doubleday/Currency.

[8] Duckworth, A. (2016). Grit: The Power of Passion and Perseverance. Scribner.

[9] Drucker, P. F. (1980). Managing in Turbulent Times. Harper & Row.

[10] Nadella, S. (2017). Hit Refresh: The Quest to Rediscover Microsoft's Soul and Imagine a Better Future for Everyone. HarperBusiness.

[11] Gaiman, N. (2012). University of the Arts Commencement Speech.

[12] Dweck, C. S. (2006). Mindset: The New Psychology of Success. Random House.

# Conclusion: Your Journey to Standing Out and Getting Ahead

Congratulations! You've made it to the end of "Stand Out! 15 No-Hype Strategies; Get Noticed and Get Ahead." By now, you're armed with a powerful toolkit of strategies to elevate your professional game and carve out your unique path to success. But as any seasoned traveler knows, reaching the end of a guidebook is just the beginning of the real adventure.

## The Power of Integration

As you reflect on the 15 strategies we've explored, you might be wondering, "Where do I start?" The beauty of these strategies is that they're not isolated techniques, but interconnected practices that reinforce and amplify each other. Let's take a moment to see how they weave together:

1. Developing a unique skill or expertise (Chapter 1) naturally leads to opportunities to write articles or create content (Chapter 10).

2. Consistently delivering high-quality work (Chapter 2) is a cornerstone of practicing exceptional customer service (Chapter 14).

3. Being punctual and reliable (Chapter 3) is essential when you volunteer for challenging projects (Chapter 6).

4. Active listening and empathy (Chapter 4) are crucial skills for mentoring others in your field (Chapter 11).

5. Maintaining a professional online presence (Chapter 5) goes hand in hand with cultivating a strong personal brand (Chapter 7).

The list goes on. Each strategy you implement will create a ripple effect, enhancing your ability to execute the others more effectively.

## The Journey of Continuous Improvement

Standing out and getting ahead isn't a destination—it's a journey of continuous improvement. As you work on these strategies, you'll find that there's always room for growth, always a new level to reach. This ties directly into our final strategy of cultivating a growth mindset and adaptability (Chapter 15).

Remember, as Carol Dweck says, "Becoming is better than being" [1]. Embrace the process of becoming better, of constantly refining your skills and expanding your capabilities. This mindset will not only help you stand out but will also make your professional journey more fulfilling and enjoyable.

## Overcoming Challenges

As you implement these strategies, you'll inevitably face challenges. You might feel overwhelmed trying to work on all 15 strategies at once. You might encounter setbacks or moments of self-doubt. This is all part of the process.

Here are a few tips to help you navigate these challenges:

1. **Start Small**: Choose one or two strategies to focus on initially. As you build confidence and see results, gradually incorporate more.

2. **Celebrate Small Wins**: Acknowledge your progress, no matter how small. Each step forward is a victory.

3. **Seek Support**: Share your goals with colleagues, friends, or a mentor. They can provide encouragement, accountability, and valuable feedback.

4. **Be Patient**: Remember, standing out is a marathon, not a sprint. Give yourself time to grow and improve.

5. **Learn from Setbacks**: When things don't go as planned, treat it as a learning opportunity. Ask yourself, "What can I learn from this experience?"

## The Compounding Effect

One of the most exciting aspects of implementing these strategies is the compounding effect they can have on your career. Just as compound interest can dramatically grow your financial investments over time, consistently applying these strategies can lead to exponential growth in your professional life.

For example:
- Developing a unique skill (Chapter 1) might lead to opportunities to speak at industry events (Chapter 13).
- This increased visibility could expand your professional network (Chapter 8).
- Your growing network might connect you with a mentor who helps you take on more challenging projects (Chapter 6).

- Success in these projects could lead to career advancement opportunities.

Before you know it, you've created a positive feedback loop of growth and opportunity.

## Adapting to the Future of Work

As we wrap up, it's worth noting that the professional landscape is constantly evolving. The strategies we've discussed are designed to be timeless, but the ways in which you apply them may need to adapt to changing circumstances.

For instance:
- The rise of remote work might change how you network strategically (Chapter 8) or maintain a professional online presence (Chapter 5).
- Advancements in AI and automation might influence which unique skills you choose to develop (Chapter 1).
- The increasing pace of change in many industries makes continuous education (Chapter 12) and adaptability (Chapter 15) more crucial than ever.

Stay alert to these changes, but don't be intimidated by them. With your toolkit of strategies and your growth mindset, you're well-equipped to navigate whatever the future of work may bring.

## Your Unique Path

As you move forward, remember that standing out doesn't mean being the loudest or the most aggressive. It's about authentically showcasing your unique value, consistently delivering excellence, and continually growing and adapting.

Your path to standing out will be as unique as you are. You might find that some strategies resonate more strongly with you than others. That's perfectly okay. Use this book as a guide, but trust your instincts and adapt these strategies to fit your personality, values, and goals.

## The Ripple Effect

Finally, as you implement these strategies and begin to stand out in your career, remember that your success has the power to positively impact others. By mentoring others (Chapter 11), sharing your expertise (Chapter 10), and practicing exceptional service (Chapter 14), you're not just advancing your own career—you're contributing to the growth and success of those around you.

In the words of leadership expert John C. Maxwell, "One is too small a number to achieve greatness" [2]. As you rise, bring others with you. Your legacy won't just be in your individual achievements, but in the positive influence you have on your colleagues, your industry, and perhaps even your community.

## Your Next Step

So, where do you go from here? The answer is simple: forward. Choose a strategy that resonates with you and take one small action today to implement it. Maybe it's updating your LinkedIn profile, volunteering for a new project at work, or signing up for an online course to develop a new skill.

Remember, the journey of a thousand miles begins with a single step. You've already taken that step by reading this book. Now, it's time to put these strategies into action.

As you close this book and step back into your professional life, carry with you the knowledge that you have everything you need to stand out and get ahead. The strategies are in your hands, the potential is within you, and the future is yours to shape.

Go forth, stand out, and make your unique mark on the professional world. Your journey to standing out and getting ahead starts now. Embrace it, enjoy it, and let your light shine!

---

References:

[1] Dweck, C. S. (2006). Mindset: The New Psychology of Success. Random House.

[2] Maxwell, J. C. (2008). Teamwork 101: What Every Leader Needs to Know. Thomas Nelson.

Dear Reader:

Thanks for taking the time to read this book.  I hope you found it beneficial and gave you practical ways to significantly improve your life.  That was my goal in writing it.

If you enjoyed it, you'll particularly like others in the Keys of Knowledge series.

Click "Follow" on my Author Page to be notified of new releases.

About the Author:

H. Bradley Stucki has been a director in three different investment companies, a Senior Vice President at a bank, and owns three businesses.

He helped pioneer the concept of "Business Incubation" and worked with over 250 fledgling companies helping them grow and flourish while still early in his career.

He was born and raised in southern Utah with horses, cows, and other assorted pets.  He is the third of six children and survived childhood only by utilizing an active imagination. His hobbies include reading and travel.